A gay guy's guide to

~~life~~

love

food

Khanh Ong

TO MY MUM, DZUNG, MY LATE DAD, TAM, AND MY SISTER, AMY. i LOVE YOU.

TO EVERY FOODIE, HOME COOK AND READER. SHARE THESE RECIPES AND THE LOVE.

TO MY EX-BOYFRIENDS AND LOVERS WHO ARE STRANGERS NOW ... LOL. i PROBS WROTE ABOUT YOU iN THiS BOOK AND CHANGED YOUR NAME. SORRY ABOUT THAT.
P.S. i'M WINNING.

A gay guy's guide to

~~life~~ love food

OUTRAGEOUSLY DELICIOUS
RECIPES (PLUS STORIES
AND DATING ADVICE) FROM
A FOOD-OBSESSED GAY

Khanh Ong

 plum. Pan Macmillan Australia

CONTENTS

INTRODUCTION   8

COOK'S NOTES   12

CHAPTER ONE 17 HERITAGE SECRETS

VIETNAMESE DISHES FROM MY CHILDHOOD

CHAPTER TWO 63 THE FAMILY WE CHOOSE

COOKING FOR (AND WITH!) YOUR FRIENDS

A BROKEN HEART   CHAPTER THREE 101

FOOD TO PICK YOU UP AFTER YOU'VE FALLEN

CHAPTER
FOUR
143

SUSTAINABLE
DATING

EASY MEALS THAT
LOOK IMPRESSIVE AF
AND TASTE YUM

CHAPTER
FIVE
185

BEING
BASIC

SIMPLE AND
HEALTHY EATS
FOR EVERY DAY

CONVERSION CHARTS   230
THANK YOU!   232
INDEX   234

INTRODUCTION

Hi :D

I'm Khanh. You may know me from *Masterchef Australia* 2018 and 2020 ... cute, right? Besides that I'm so much more, so let's go through my resume. I'm a single gay man with my own bar and restaurant, The George on Collins in Melbourne (go there, it's lit), a presenter on a national TV show, a sometimes DJ (no requests ... soz) and an all-the-time cook. This is my guide to life, love and FOOD.

Food is the love of my life, and that love began in childhood. My parents came to Australia in the early 1990s after spending four years in an immigration camp in Indonesia where I was born. I grew up in a very Vietnamese household in an even more Vietnamese area in south-east Melbourne. Surrounded by beautiful food and produce, I found myself cooking with my mum and learning all about flavour (I was really just eating things I thought were yummy, but that's still learning, right?).

'I'VE GONE THROUGH A FEW CAREER CHANGES, FROM FASHION TO DESIGN TO MUSIC, BUT THE CONSTANT HAS ALWAYS BEEN FOOD.'

My love affair with food continued in my teens when my family opened a butcher and I began to learn about working with animals and cooking meat. With both parents working long hours, I would love it when Mum came home from the shop to prepare dinner, and I spent a lot of time after school watching her cook. It was our special time together and to this day it remains one of my fondest memories.

In my late teens I lost my dad to cancer and my mum had less time to cook, so I kinda took over those duties. I've gone through a few career changes, from fashion to design to music, but the constant has always been food. Food is my happy place, it reminds me of all the good times. I cook banh xeo or pho bo and think of Dad, or I eat prawns and pork belly and remember after-school meals with my sister. I love how food is able to transport you to a time, place or feeling. Anyway, enough of the sappy stuff.

To be honest, just like you I'm trying to balance my work, social life, family life and everything in between, while keeping myself open for love. I wrote this book because I wanted to remind you how important food is in keeping a healthy balance. There's no good or bad, this book is all about how food makes you feel, how it brings your friends and family together and how it helps you connect with others.

In the coming pages, you will find five super-sexy chapters, everything from family recipes and food for your friends, to dishes that will make you feel good after a break-up, perfect meals for a date and the basics that everyone should have up their sleeve. I've got you covered for whatever point of the emotional rollercoaster known as life that you are on. Sometimes that rollercoaster speeds up and then slows down a few dozen times a day, but let's leave my mental breakdowns for another time.

Heritage Secrets are family recipes that I've picked Mum's and Grandma's brains for. It doesn't get any more authentic than this. There are meals I've eaten all my life, some insanely delicious street food and dishes my mum now refuses to make for me (mainly because she can't be bothered anymore).

The Family We Choose is filled with dishes for the people who may not actually be related to you but are your ride or die; this is the food you want to share with those who make up your support system. These dishes remind me of my nearest and dearest, the people who I can completely read to filth because they know how much I love them.

A Broken Heart can be devastating sometimes and inspiring at other times. Whatever way you want to grieve, I have recipes to help you through it; whether you want healthy, hearty or the perfect sugar hit, I've got you covered. Let's eat our feelings, whatever they may be.

Sustainable Dating ... what even is that? I don't know, but I do know how to cook for dates of all types. Wanna look uber impressive but actually not do too much? I'll help you wizard your way into the heart of any potential partner. Dating advice may be offered here too, but I also suggest you don't take it from a single man ... hahahaha.

Being Basic is all about taking things back to ground level, to where you are cooking and eating to stay alive – but that doesn't mean you don't deserve banging flavour. Let's tackle the fundamentals together and pump out a tasty feed.

Food for me is about being simple and delicious – just like life. You'll find a lot of easy and approachable dishes in this book. I find cooking for some people can be intimidating, so I wanted to cut that out. Let's have fun, cook yummy food and pretend we slaved away all day in the kitchen when in actual fact it took 30 minutes. I'll show you how to not over-complicate things and still be able to punch in heaps of flavour and keep eating interesting.

OKAY, ENOUGH FLUFF ... LET'S COOK!

COOK'S NOTES

Just like handwriting, we all have our own unique style of cooking. It may seem foreign and strange to some people, but your cooking style is part of your personality and your voice. So, here are a few notes to help explain some of *my* quirks in the kitchen – the ways in which I use particular ingredients, favourite pieces of equipment, that kind of thing. I hope these notes make it easier to navigate this book so that you can spend more time cooking, having fun and feeding your loved ones.

- Oven temperatures are conventional, unless otherwise stated.

- I always use sea salt flakes and keep a large bowl of it on hand in my kitchen. I find sea salt less harsh and lighter in flavour, making it harder to over-season your food.

- Growing up in a Vietnamese family, I learned to never deseed my chillies. I love the heat that comes from them, but feel free to deseed or reduce the amount of chilli in these recipes if you're not into a lot of spice.

- I know that many people don't like the outer leaves of lemongrass, but I've always used three-quarters of the way up the stalk and not just the white bits, so unless specified feel free to do the same.

- At home I generally cook multiple dishes that you can pick and choose from, share style (especially Vietnamese dishes), so a lot of these recipes are great as a starter, side or as part of a small banquet.

- These recipes, like all recipes, are meant to be used as a guide. I would love for everyone to follow them step by step, but feel free to adapt and change ingredients; for example, if you don't like cabbage then swap it out. Work out if the ingredient is there for flavour, texture or colour and sub in similar things that you like. Cooking is supposed to be enjoyable; it's not meant to be stressful or confusing. Take chances, try new things and have fun.

- I believe everyone should have a charcoal barbecue at home! They are readily available at hardware stores and you can actually buy the coal from most supermarkets. There are some great portable options that can easily sit on a benchtop, and they are so easy to use. I love using a charcoal barbecue to make some of my favourite Vietnamese street food dishes, like grilled scallops with spring onion oil (page 25) or charred marinated pork (page 218). I keep mine outside just because the clean up is easier. Grab one, use it for everything and I guarantee your food will taste so much better.

- If you don't want to start up the charcoal barbecue, I suggest buying a blow torch. For me, it's a must-have, as it can easily mimic a barbecue's smoky flavour and it also looks cool AF.

Essential ingredients

When I was growing up, my pantry was so different to my friends', but I feel that Australians have become much more open minded about cooking with ingredients from other cuisines. I've popped some of my essentials below – fill your kitchen with these and you'll be able to whip up most of my dishes. You'll find these ingredients at Asian grocers or supermarkets.

Pantry and benchtop

- **Aromatics.** Shallots, ginger, galangal, onions, garlic, lemongrass and assorted chillies can always be found in a bowl on my benchtop next to my fruit bowl.

- **Oils.** I always stock extra-virgin olive, vegetable, grapeseed, coconut and peanut oil. I also make my own chilli oil by heating grapeseed oil in a small saucepan, then adding dried chilli flakes, star anise and cinnamon sticks and leaving it to infuse.

- **Sauces and vinegars.** You'll need soy sauce, fish sauce, vinegars (rice wine, white and balsamic), oyster sauce, mirin, cooking sake, shaoxing (Chinese cooking wine), sesame oil and kecap manis (heavs).

- **Spices.** Must-haves are ground turmeric, coriander, cumin, cinnamon and ginger, as well as smoked paprika, star anise, onion powder, garlic powder and chilli powder.

Fridge

- **Herbs.** I always keep a container of herbs wrapped in a damp cloth (Chux or something similar) in my fridge. These herbs include coriander, mint, Vietnamese mint (must have!), dill, parsley, spring onions and basil.

- **Makrut lime leaves.** I store these in my container of herbs, but just a note on the name. As the word kaffir is offensive in some cultures, I've chosen to use its alternative name in this book.

- **Condiments and sauces.** Sriracha chilli sauce, tomato sauce, Tabasco, homemade nuoc mam dipping sauce (page 34), hoisin sauce, sambals, miso, mustard, kewpie mayo and peanut butter are my essentials.

- **Other basics.** I also stock my fridge with good butter, cream, pickles and pickled ground chilli.

SAUCY!

CHAPTER ONE

HERITAGE SECRETS

VIETNAMESE DISHES FROM
MY CHILDHOOD

My family, heritage and childhood really were the building blocks that helped me become the man I am today. I owe everything to my parents, who immigrated to Australia in the early 1990s to build a better life for us all. They took a massive risk by leaving their home, where they were comfortable, protected and had the support of their family. To them I owe everything.

My parents weren't your stereotypical Vietnamese parents. They supported EVERY endeavour and idea that I had, whether it was wanting to go to fashion school, sing, play drums, go into theatre, play water polo, study photography, be a plastic surgeon (yes, this was a career option I considered when I was 16 years old!), own a nightclub (also a dream when I was 16; side note: I kinda own one now) or be a DJ. They supported me to do anything I wanted as long as I was happy, and for this I am so thankful. They allowed me to explore, grow and figure out what I wanted (and didn't want) from life.

My mum (Dzung) and dad (Tam) started their own butcher when I was eight years old, both working seven days a week to provide for me and my younger sister (Amy – we love her). I remember my mum would always come home an hour or so before dad to cook us dinner (cute, right?). Whether she was making chicken noodle soup, sweet and sour squid or Hue-style beef noodle soup, she would do it all from scratch. Being a curious and bright-eyed little boy, I would buzz around like an annoying mosquito in the kitchen watching her. I think this is where I fell in love with food. I really enjoyed my nights with Mum, chopping daikon, peeling carrots and sneakily stealing anything that was ready to nibble on before dinner. I learned a lot over the next decade, helping mum every night. At the time it sometimes felt like a chore, but looking back now, I think it was my favourite part of the day. I don't remember fights at school or playground chat, but I do remember coming home in the afternoon and having freshly cooked rice with school prawns and pork belly.

This chapter is about my core, the dishes I grew up eating and loving, dishes that remind me of home, of Vietnam and of being a child. These recipes range from quick and simple 15-minute meals to broths that you will pour your heart into and spend half a day cooking because, well, they are worth it. You'll find wonderful family recipes (stolen from my mum), adaptations of my favourite street dishes and recipes that I've made up that just remind me of my mum's cooking.

WHAT'S IN THIS CHAPTER?

♡ HERE YOU'LL FIND MY ROOTS IN VIETNAMESE COOKING. THIS IS THE FOOD I CRAVE AFTER BEING AWAY FOR A WEEK AND THE FOOD I BEG MY MUM TO MAKE FOR ME WHEN I VISIT.

♡ VIETNAMESE MUST-HAVES, FROM MILKY ICED COFFEE (PAGE 20) TO CHICKEN NOODLE SOUP (PAGE 52), CRISPY VIETNAMESE PANCAKES (PAGE 37) AND TAMARIND CRAB (PAGE 50). THESE ARE THE DISHES THAT KEEP ME JETTING BACK TO VIETNAM (LEGIT ANY EXCUSE WILL DO THOUGH).

♡ THIS FOOD IS A CELEBRATION OF MY BACKGROUND AND I HOPE YOU LOVE THESE RECIPES. OKAY, ENOUGH OF THE SAPPY STUFF, TURN THE PAGE FOR MY FAVOURITE CAFFEINE KICK.

VIETNAMESE ICED COFFEE AKA the BEST COFFEE in the WORLD

CA PHE SUA DA

Ca phe sua da is extremely addictive and so easy to make. Traditionally, it's made in a coffee phin, which is a small stainless steel filtering device. The hot coffee drips through the filter onto a glass of ice, emitting the most wonderful aromas, which go so well with the condensed milk. This shit is so good, I'm legit craving it as I write. You can cheat if you don't have a phin filter by using espresso, but this process is so worth it – plus the filters are cheap and easy to find at your Asian grocer.

SERVES 1

- 1 cup ice cubes
- 2 tablespoons Vietnamese ground coffee or other medium-grind coffee
- 125 ml (½ cup) boiling water that's been left to cool down for 1 minute (you want the water to be around 90°C)
- 1–2 tablespoons sweetened condensed milk

Pop the ice into a serving glass. Place your Vietnamese coffee phin over the top of the glass and spoon the coffee into the phin.

Add the cooled boiled water then pop the lid on the phin and watch as the coffee drips onto the ice. Leave to fully filter through – this will usually take about 4 minutes. Once finished, add a tablespoon or two of sweetened condensed milk depending on how sweet you like your coffee.

TIP: USUALLY THE ICE STOPS ALL OF THE CONDENSED MILK FROM DISSOLVING. IN VIETNAM, ONCE WE'RE HALFWAY DONE DRINKING OUR COFFEE, WE LIKE TO TOP IT UP WITH GREEN TEA FOR A SWEET MIX OF TEA AND COFFEE.

STREETSIDE CORN on THE COB

BAP NUONG MO HANH

Make your way through Southeast Asia and you'll find versions of this dish being sold from little carts and makeshift barbecues in alleyways. My housemate, Diana, asked me about this corn while she was in Vietnam, not understanding why it wasn't sweet. I explained that in Vietnam this dish is usually made with a soft, pale variety of corn that is eaten for its almost powder-like texture, not for its sweetness. My preference though, is the yellow sweet corn we get here in Australia. The addition of nutritional yeast really dials up the umami flavour to 100. If you're not opposed to dairy, you can easily sub in a wonderful parmesan.

SERVES 4

4 sweet corn cobs, husks left on
3 tablespoons Spring Onion Oil
    (page 25)
2 tablespoons nutritional yeast
sea salt, to taste

Heat a barbecue grill (preferably charcoal) to high or a chargrill pan over high heat.

Peel the husks back from the corn and discard. Tie them using a piece of the husk to create a handle. Snip off any straggly ends of the husk.

Place the corn onto the grill and cook on all sides for about 8 minutes, until charred and blistering.

Remove the corn from the grill and top with the spring onion oil, nutritional yeast and salt.

Grab the corn by its handle and chow down.

TIP: SPRING ONION
OIL IS A GREAT HOME
STAPLE AND YOU'LL
SEE IT USED A FEW MORE
TIMES THROUGHOUT THIS BOOK
BECAUSE IT'S SO VERSATILE. IT'S
EASY TO MAKE IN BULK, JUST DOUBLE
OR TRIPLE THE RECIPE.

GRILLED SCALLOPS with SPRING ONION OIL

DIEP NUONG MO HANH

Diep nuong mo hanh, or grilled scallops with spring onion oil, is a simple and widely loved dish in the Vietnamese community. As a people, we eat shellfish by the bucketload due to its abundance in Vietnam. In Ho Chi Minh City, you'll find little streetside stalls where you can choose your snails, clams or other sea life to be prepared, with a sauce of your choice, right in front of you. It's really cute to sit on those tiny little plastic stools while you wait. They always look too flimsy to hold your weight, but I haven't broken one yet! The scallops in this recipe are interchangeable with other molluscs, such as mussels, clams or oysters, and I've even had baby abalone prepared this way. Grilling really brings the sweetness from the shellfish to life and the hint of smokiness you get from the juices hitting the coals is to die for.

SERVES 4

12 scallops in the half shell
40 g (¼ cup) crushed Salted Peanuts
 (page 26)
2 tablespoons crispy fried shallots
pinch of sea salt
2 long red chillies, finely sliced
 (optional)

SPRING ONION OIL
10 spring onions, green part only,
 finely sliced
200 ml vegetable oil
½ teaspoon sea salt

To make the spring onion oil, place all the ingredients in a saucepan over medium heat. Bring to a simmer and cook for 2–3 minutes until the spring onion starts to soften. Set aside to cool. You probably won't use all of the oil for this recipe, so pop any leftovers in an airtight container and keep in the fridge for up to 1 week.

Heat a barbecue grill plate to medium, preferably over charcoal. If using charcoal, wait until the coals have had an initial burn and have started to die down.

Cook the scallops on the half shell for 1–2 minutes until the scallops are bubbling in their own juices. Watch as the scallops become a little firmer and smaller, changing from opaque to a milky white colour. Add 1 teaspoon of the spring onion oil to each scallop and continue to cook for a further 1–2 minutes. Depending on the size of your barbecue, you may have to cook the scallops in batches.

Remove the scallops to a serving tray and finish by topping each with 1 teaspoon of crushed peanuts, a sprinkling of crispy shallots, a pinch of salt and, if you'd like a fresh hit of heat, add a couple of slices of red chilli.

BEEF WRAPPED in BETEL LEAF

BO LA LOT

You can smell beef wrapped in betel leaf cooking from a mile away. The mouth-watering aroma and, as you get closer, the sound of the meat sizzling, is mesmerising. This dish is complemented by salted peanuts, traditionally cooked up to the brink of their existence. The nuts, bordering on burnt, are just bitter enough to contrast with the sweetness of the beef and the floral notes in the aromatics.

SERVES 2–4 (DEPENDING ON IF YOU'RE A NORMAL PERSON OR ME, BECAUSE I EAT THESE AS THEY'RE COOKING AND RARELY LEAVE ANY BEHIND)

500 g beef mince (the fattier the better)
150 g pork mince
2 lemongrass stalks, white part only, finely chopped
6 spring onions, white part only, finely chopped
½ bunch of coriander, roots scraped clean, roots and stems finely chopped (save the leaves for another use)
2 garlic cloves, finely chopped
1 red shallot, finely chopped
1½ teaspoons caster sugar
1 teaspoon ground white pepper
1 tablespoon fish sauce
pinch of sea salt
40 betel leaves with stems attached (see Tip)
Spring Onion Oil (page 25), to serve

SALTED PEANUTS
1 tablespoon sea salt
150 g shelled and skinned whole raw peanuts

To make the salted peanuts, combine the salt with 3 tablespoons of water and mix until dissolved. Toast the peanuts in a dry frying pan over high heat for 8–10 minutes until golden and almost charred. Add the salted water to the pan 1 tablespoon at a time, stirring with a wooden spoon and waiting for the water to evaporate before adding more. Set aside to cool, then roughly chop. You can make the salted peanuts ahead of time (or just to keep on hand as a snack). They'll keep in an airtight container for up to 2 weeks.

Soak 10 bamboo skewers in warm water for 20 minutes (or use metal skewers). Get your barbecue or charcoal grill nice and hot.

In a large mixing bowl, pop all the ingredients besides the betel leaves and spring onion oil and mix well. Leave to marinate for 15 minutes.

Trim the betel leaf stems, leaving 1 cm attached to the leaf. Place a betel leaf on a clean surface with the shiny side facing down. Place 1 heaped tablespoon of the beef mixture onto the leaf near the pointy end. Fold in the sides and roll towards the stem. Use the stem to pierce the leaf and secure the roll. Pop a skewer crossways through the middle of the roll. Repeat with the rest of the leaves and mixture, placing four rolls on each skewer.

Cook the rolls on the preheated barbecue grill for 2 minutes on each side until nice and charred.

To serve, top the skewers with lots of spring onion oil and chopped salted peanuts.

TIP: BETEL LEAVES ARE VINE LEAVES WITH BITTER, PEPPERY FLAVOUR NOTES. THEY ARE SOLD FRESH IN MOST ASIAN GROCERS AND SOME GOOD GREENGROCERS.

WRAP, SKEWER, GRILL, DEVOUR!

FIVE-SPICE SCHOOL PRAWNS

TOM RANG NGU VI HUONG

Five-spice – famously known as Chinese five-spice – is actually a vital part of Vietnamese cooking: we call it ngu vi huong. Five-spice adds an essential aromatic, moreish hum to many dishes. School prawns are a mouth-watering favourite of mine and this recipe, as unconventional as it is due to the addition of smoked paprika, has even been adopted into my mum's repertoire. Perfect for an afternoon in the sun with lime mayo for dipping and an icy cold beer, cider or Bucha Brothers alcoholic kombucha (little plug for my bestie Tara's business, wink wink*).

SERVES 2

50 g rice flour
50 g cornflour
1½ teaspoons Chinese five-spice
1 teaspoon smoked paprika
sea salt
500 g raw school prawns, heads removed, tails and legs trimmed to get rid of any sharp bits
neutral oil for deep-frying (such as vegetable oil)
100 g dried whole red chillies

LIME MAYO
zest of 2 limes, plus lime wedges to serve
90 g (⅓ cup) 2-Minute Mayo (page 151)

To make the lime mayo, mix the zest with the mayo and set aside.

Place the rice flour, cornflour, five-spice, paprika and ½ teaspoon of salt in a large bowl and combine well.

Spread the school prawns on some paper towel and pat dry.

Fill a large deep saucepan about one-third full with oil and heat to 180°C or until a cube of bread dropped in the oil browns in 15 seconds. Pop a quarter of the school prawns into the flour mixture along with a quarter of the chillies. Toss to coat and shake off any excess flour.

Carefully add the school prawns and chillies to the oil and fry for 1½–2 minutes until golden and crispy. Remove the prawns and chillies from the fryer and drain on paper towel. Repeat with the remaining prawns and chillies.

Sprinkle with salt flakes and serve hot, with the lime mayo for dipping and lime wedges for squeezing over.

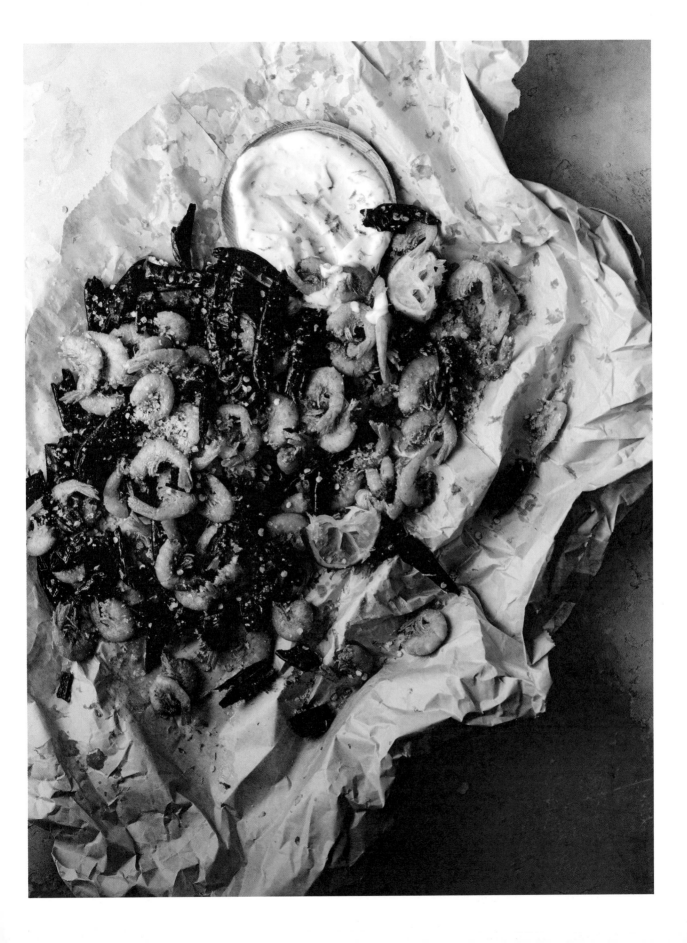

TIP: IF YOU PREFER A DIFFERENT
DIPPING SAUCE, A LITTLE SOY OR
SWEET CHILLI SAUCE WOULD ALSO DO!

PRAWN and PORK SPRING ROLLS

CHA GIO TOM THIT

Spring rolls are divine. If you don't like them, sorry, you're a psychopath. NOW, when I was younger, Mum would have bags of these in the freezer ready for any entertaining emergency, but she kinda stopped after I moved out of home when she found out I was just raiding the freezer every time I visited and taking them home ... sorry Mum for being a poor uni student <eye roll emoji>. It got to the point where she refused to make them, so I had to steal her recipe and now I make bags of them for my freezer. I'm hoping you will, too, because you can fry them directly from frozen – just add another 60–90 seconds of cooking time.

SERVES 2-4

300 g pork mince
2 eggs
1 teaspoon caster sugar
½ teaspoon freshly ground
 black pepper
1 small carrot, finely grated
50 g black fungus or wood ear
 mushrooms, finely shredded
3 small red shallots, finely chopped
1 garlic clove, crushed
2 teaspoons fish sauce
pinch of sea salt
16 spring roll wrappers
16 raw prawns, peeled and
 deveined, leaving the tails intact
neutral oil for deep-frying (such as
 vegetable oil)

TO SERVE

fresh herbs, such as coriander,
 mint and Vietnamese mint
iceberg lettuce leaves
Nuoc Mam Dipping Sauce (page 34)

In a large mixing bowl, place the pork mince, 1 egg, the sugar, pepper, carrot, mushroom, shallot, garlic, fish sauce and salt. Mix well.

In a small bowl, beat the remaining egg – you'll use this to bind the wrapped spring rolls.

Place a spring roll wrapper on a clean work surface with a corner pointing towards you. Keep the remaining wrappers covered while you work so they don't dry out. Spoon a heaped teaspoon of the pork mixture near the corner closest to you and spread the mixture one-third of the way up and across the middle third of the wrapper. Fold the left and right corners in so they overlap the mixture. Now place a prawn on the mixture so that the tail sticks out over one of the folded edges. Brush the top third of the wrapper with the egg wash and, starting with the corner closest to you, tightly roll the wrapper around the prawn and seal well.

Repeat with the remaining wrappers, pork mixture and prawns. You should end up with 16 spring rolls.

Fill a small saucepan to about one-third full with oil and heat to 180°C or until a cube of bread dropped in the oil browns in 15 seconds.

Working in batches of three or four (you don't want to overcrowd the pan), fry the spring rolls for 3–4 minutes, turning occasionally, until golden and crisp. Carefully remove and drain on paper towel.

Serve hot with piles of fresh herbs and lettuce leaves. To eat, pop a spring roll into a lettuce leaf, add some herbs, roll it up and dip this delicious little parcel into the nuoc mam.

NUOC MAM DIPPING SAUCE

NUOC MAM

Nuoc mam dipping sauce – commonly called nuoc mam – is the most famous Vietnamese sauce and it's served with almost everything. Nuoc mam means fish sauce in Vietnamese. Mum used to tell me how in Vietnam a bride is judged by the groom's family on how well she makes nuoc mam. Look, I don't know how strict this way of vetting is, but it's a cute little story. The sauce has to be a perfect balance of sweet, sour and salty. I tend to make this by the litre and have it ready to go in the fridge. It keeps for ages due to the high acid level, sugar and fish sauce, which kind of makes it a bit like a pickle.

MAKES ABOUT 150 ML

- 3 tablespoons warm water
- 1 tablespoon caster sugar, plus extra if needed
- juice of 1 lime, plus extra if needed
- 2 tablespoons fish sauce, plus extra if needed
- 2 garlic cloves, finely chopped, plus extra if needed
- 3 bird's eye chillies, finely chopped, plus extra if needed

Mix the water and sugar in a bowl until the sugar has dissolved.

Add the lime juice and fish sauce to the sugar water and give it a stir. Now add the garlic and chilli.

Taste your nuoc mam – it should be sweet, sour and salty, with a kick of chilli. Add a little more of any of the ingredients until the sauce is perfectly balanced.

TIP: TOSS THIS DIPPING SAUCE THROUGH YOUR FAVOURITE SALAD WITH HERBS LIKE MINT OR BASIL TO BOOST THE YUM FACTOR.

I WOULD SWIM
IN THIS IF I COULD

CRISPY VIETNAMESE PANCAKES

BANH XEO

Banh xeo are crispy, savoury, turmeric and coconut-based plates of heaven and so moreish due to the perfect balance of salty, sweet and umami flavours. The herbs boost the freshness level and really bring everything together. Feel free to play around with different fillings, too – you can use chicken, tofu or mung beans. Just like breakfast pancakes, the first one you make is usually a dud, so don't be disheartened. My mum never enjoyed making banh xeo for us, because we would chow down on them straight off the wok as she cooked them, so she would never get to eat with the fam when she made these.

SERVES 4

175 g (1 cup) rice flour
2 tablespoons cornflour
400 ml canned coconut milk
250 ml (1 cup) iced water
2 teaspoons ground turmeric
1 teaspoon caster sugar
2 spring onions, finely sliced
sea salt
250 g boneless pork belly,
    finely sliced
150 g raw tiger prawns, peeled,
    deveined and chopped
1 onion, finely sliced
1 tablespoon fish sauce
2 teaspoons ground white pepper
3 tablespoons peanut oil
45 g (½ cup) bean sprouts

TO SERVE
Nuoc Mam Dipping Sauce (page 34)
lettuce leaves
½ bunch of Vietnamese mint
½ bunch of coriander
½ bunch of mint

Mix the rice flour, cornflour, coconut milk, water, turmeric, sugar, spring onion and ½ teaspoon of salt in a large mixing bowl to make a smooth batter. Set aside for 20 minutes to allow the batter to develop.

Meanwhile, in another mixing bowl, combine the pork belly, prawn, onion, fish sauce, pepper and a pinch of salt and leave to marinate for 30 minutes.

Heat a large wok over high heat and add 2 teaspoons of the peanut oil. Once the oil is hot (just before it starts to smoke), add 2 tablespoons of the pork belly mixture and cook for 2 minutes. Add a ladleful of the batter and roll it around the wok to spread the mixture thinly like a pancake. Turn the heat down and cook on low for about 5 minutes, then place a small handful of the bean sprouts over the banh xeo. Cover with a lid and cook for 1 minute, then remove the lid and cook for another 2 minutes until the edge of the banh xeo is crispy and coming away from the wok. Using a spatula, carefully fold the banh xeo in half, remove from the wok and tip onto a platter. This is your first banh xeo done, now repeat with the remaining pork mixture and batter. You should be able to make four.

Serve on a platter with nuoc mam on the side for dipping, and a big pile of lettuce leaves and herbs.

TIP: EAT THIS LIKE A DIY LETTUCE WRAP. BREAK UP SOME OF THE BANH XEO ONTO A LETTUCE LEAF TOPPED WITH FRESH HERBS. ROLL IT UP AND GIVE IT A DIP IN THE NUOC MAM.

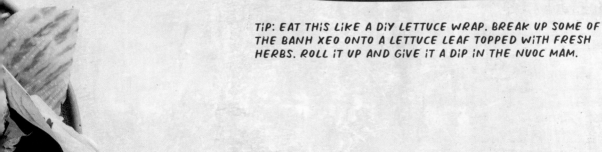

CRISPY
VIETNAMESE
PANCAKES
(PAGE 37)

LITTLE PLATES OF HEAVEN

STIR-FRIED WATER SPINACH with GARLIC

RAU MUONG XAO TOI

All through high school I pretty much lived off rau muong, so it was a no-brainer for this dish to make it onto my restaurant menu and into this book. Known in Australia by many names, such as water spinach and morning glory (lol), this vegetable is a favourite in many Asian households, although when it hits $25 a kilo I usually pass and wait for it to come back down to the more affordable $4 a kilo. At home, my sister and I always fought over the leaves, whereas my dad loved the stems for their satisfying mouthfeel.

SERVES 4

1 bunch (about 700 g) of water spinach, washed thoroughly and drained, stems trimmed
2 tablespoons vegetable oil
2 tablespoons roughly chopped garlic
1 long red chilli, finely sliced
1 teaspoon fish sauce
2 teaspoons light soy sauce
1 teaspoon ground white pepper
pinch of sea salt

Tear the leaves from the water spinach and cut the stems into finger-length pieces. Set aside separately.

Heat a large wok over high heat. Add the oil, garlic and chilli and cook for 30 seconds or until the garlic turns golden. Add the water spinach stems and cook, stirring, for 3 minutes. Add the leaves and cook for 2 minutes or until the leaves wilt. Add the fish sauce, soy sauce, pepper and salt and cook, stirring, for 1 minute.

Transfer to a serving dish and eat straight away.

HERITAGE SECRETS: VIETNAMESE DISHES FROM MY CHILDHOOD

HIT ME WITH FOOD QUESTIONS

DEATH ROW MEAL?

HERE GOES ... (i DON'T CARE iF i CAN ONLY HAVE A BiTE OF EACH.)

- 3 Wicked Wings
- Truffle mac and cheese
- Mum's bun bo Hue and pipis
- Cacio e pepe
- 2 pieces of Korean fried chicken
- Simple pecorino and rocket salad
- Half a dozen oysters
- 1 blue swimmer crab
- 1 rib eye with chimichurri
- 1 slice of wood-fired pepperoni pizza
- Chicken and sweet corn soup
- Nando's chips from the fryer with extra peri peri
- Grilled occy over a fire
- Charred brussels sprouts
- Mangosteen
- My fave aged high-altitude gruyere
- Cold iceberg lettuce

WTF!

OMG, BUT ALSO:

- Bun rieu
- Banh bot loc
- Potato on the stick thing
- Tiny chicken sandwiches you get at high tea
- Fairy bread

SOS

OH, BUT IF I WAS REALLY ON DEATH ROW AND I WANTED PEOPLE TO BE SCARED OR WEIRDED OUT BY ME, I'D ASK FOR SOMETHING LIKE SEVEN JELLY BABIES WITH THEIR HEADS CUT OFF.

TIP: LOTUS STEMS CAN BE FOUND AT ASIAN GROCERS, SOMETIMES IN THE FROZEN SECTION. IF YOU CAN'T FIND THEM, YOU CAN USE FINELY SLICED CELERY AS IT HAS A VERY SIMILAR TEXTURE, BUT THE FLAVOUR WILL DEFINITELY BE DIFFERENT, SO TRY YOUR BEST TO SOURCE THE LOTUS.

PRAWN and LOTUS STEM SALAD

GOI NGO SEN

In Vietnamese culture, the lotus flower is a symbol of purity. The seeds, stems and roots are all edible and used in a lot of Vietnamese dishes. The lotus stem has a slightly crunchy texture and a subtle flavour because it grows in fresh water. One of the things I've always loved about lotus is that something so beautiful (and delicious) can grow in such un-glam conditions. (I have a lotus mandala tattoo for this reason.)

This salad is so addictive and is usually made for dinner parties, weddings or funerals (Vietnamese funerals are massive parties to celebrate life and, after the formalities are done, huge feasts take place). This salad packs sweet, sour and umami flavours and it's so healthy too, which is always a plus. I like to serve this as a canapé, with the salad piled on top of a prawn cracker and topped with half a prawn – just make sure you don't do it too far ahead of time so the cracker stays crunchy.

SERVES 2

250 g lotus stem (see Tip)
1 long red chilli, cut into 5 cm lengths and very finely sliced
generous handful of Vietnamese mint leaves, roughly torn
150 g cooked prawns, peeled and deveined
juice of ½ lime, plus lime wedges to serve
1 teaspoon caster sugar
pinch of sea salt
80 ml (⅓ cup) Nuoc Mam Dipping Sauce (page 34)
small handful of coriander leaves
3 tablespoons roughly chopped Salted Peanuts (page 26)
2 tablespoons crispy fried shallots
sesame rice crackers or prawn crackers, to serve (optional)

Start by prepping your lotus stem. Cut three-quarters of the stems into 5 cm pieces, then halve them lengthways. Finely slice the remaining lotus stems.

In a large mixing bowl, combine the lotus stem, chilli, Vietnamese mint, prawns, lime juice, sugar and salt.

Transfer the salad to a serving bowl and coat well with the nuoc mam. Scatter over the coriander, peanuts and shallots and serve with rice or prawn crackers (if you like) and lime wedges on the side for squeezing over.

BEEF NOODLE SOUP

PHO BO

Unlike chicken noodle soup (page 52), beef noodle soup is a dish Mum really loved making. She would spend a whole day prepping and cooking, sometimes even beginning the night before (the longer you leave the broth to simmer with the bones the better it tastes). She loved inviting the extended family around to savour the liquid gold that she'd laboured away on. I didn't really understand the fuss until I did it myself. This dish requires love, attention and patience, and the end result always brings a smile to my face. The reason for the large quantities is because of how much work goes into it – there isn't much point making just enough for two. So give this a go, and invite your family, friends, neighbours and work spouse to come enjoy it because it's that pho-king good.

SERVES 8

1.5 kg beef marrow bone, cut into pieces the size of your fist (ask your butcher to do this)
1 kg beef brisket
500 g oxtail
500 g beef flank or skirt steak
3 tablespoons sea salt
2 large onions, unpeeled
2 x 6 cm pieces of ginger
4 red shallots, unpeeled
1 tablespoon coriander seeds
2 teaspoons fennel seeds
6 cloves
3 star anise
1 cinnamon stick
3 black cardamom pods, lightly crushed
3 tablespoons fish sauce
2 tablespoons rock sugar (see Tips)

TO SERVE

1 kg fresh flat rice noodles (cooked according to packet instructions)
540 g (6 cups) bean sprouts
800 g raw eye fillet or scotch fillet, very finely sliced
2 bunches of Thai basil, leaves picked
1 bunch of coriander, leaves picked
5 bunches of spring onions, finely chopped
Vinegar Onions (page 52)
sliced long red chilli
4 limes, halved
hoisin sauce
sriracha chilli sauce
pickled chilli (see Tips page 53; optional)

Place the marrow bone, brisket, oxtail and flank or skirt steak in a 15 litre stockpot. Add 2 tablespoons of the salt, cover with cold water and bring to the boil over high heat. Cook on a rolling boil for 15 minutes, then strain and discard the liquid. Rinse the meat and bones with warm water – this is to get rid of any impurities and helps keep the broth clear. Clean the stockpot and pop the rinsed bones and meat back in.

Char the onions, ginger and shallots over an open flame until the skins are black. You can do this over burning coals (ideally) or on a gas barbecue or stovetop. Using a small knife, scrape off all the black burnt bits and discard (otherwise this will colour your broth). Place the onions, ginger and shallots in the stockpot.

In a small frying pan, toast the coriander and fennel seeds, cloves, star anise, cinnamon and cardamom for 45–90 seconds until fragrant. Place the spices in a clean muslin cloth, wrap and tie tightly with kitchen string. Now chuck it into the pot with everything else.

Pour 8 litres of cold water into the pot. If it doesn't cover everything, add some more. Bring to the boil over high heat. Reduce to a simmer and cook for 2½ hours. Skim off any impurities as they rise to the surface (you'll have to do this every 30 minutes until this dish is finished cooking). Remove the brisket and flank. When the meat is cool enough, cover and place in the fridge until nearly ready to serve.

Add the fish sauce, sugar and the rest of the salt to the broth and simmer for a further 2–6 hours, remembering to skim any impurities every 30 minutes or so. The longer you simmer the broth for, the more complex and yummier the flavour will be.

When nearly ready to serve, slice the brisket and flank.

Remove the bones and strain the liquid carefully into a clean stockpot (you don't want your broth to go cloudy after all the hard work). Discard the solids. Bring the broth to a simmer when ready to serve.

HERITAGE SECRETS: VIETNAMESE DISHES FROM MY CHILDHOOD

TIPS: I'M SAYING THIS SERVES EIGHT, BUT THEY ARE EIGHT VERY GENEROUS SERVINGS, BECAUSE WHEN YOU HAVE PHO, YOU HAVE PHO. YOU NEVER LEAVE ANY PHO RESTAURANT JUST FEELING SATISFIED — YOU LEAVE EXHAUSTED, FULL TO THE BRIM, OR, AS I LIKE TO SAY, 'OMG, DYING!'. SO, WHILE THIS MIGHT COMFORTABLY FEED TWELVE, LET'S JUST CALL IT EIGHT ;)

ROCK SUGAR IS A FORM OF CRYSTALLISED SUGAR THAT COMES IN IRREGULAR SHAPED LUMPS. IT IS ALSO KNOWN AS ROCK CANDY AND IS AVAILABLE FROM ASIAN GROCERS.

To assemble, divide the noodles among eight deep bowls and top with a nice handful of bean sprouts. Add some of the sliced brisket and flank to each bowl along with 100 g of the sliced raw beef and a mixture of basil and coriander leaves and spring onion. Pour just enough simmering broth into each bowl to cover the noodles, ensuring you pour it directly on top of the raw beef, so it cooks. Finally, top with some of the vinegar onions and serve with the chilli, lime halves, hoisin, sriracha and pickled chilli on the side (if using).

AFTER-SCHOOL PRAWNS and PORK BELLY

TOM RANG THIT BA ROI

My after-school snack was always a little different from that of the average Australian. It wasn't ham-and-cheese sangers, chicken nuggets or wraps. It was rice with onion omelette, rice with pepper caramel beef, rice with prawn and pork belly or rice with fish sauce caramel fish ... you get the gist. SOOOOOOOOOOOOO, when I decided to write this book I couldn't leave out the after-school prawns and pork belly that I grew up eating. Over time, as I got bigger, so did the prawns and we always made a joke about it. Looking back, I think this was actually because my parents' businesses started doing better and our food budget increased. That said, I actually still prefer to use school prawns, even though they are smaller and cheaper.

SERVES 2

200 g boneless pork belly, finely sliced and cut into pieces about the size of the school prawns
2 tablespoons fish sauce
1 tablespoon caster sugar
3 large garlic cloves, finely chopped
1 teaspoon freshly ground black pepper
2 tablespoons vegetable oil
3 red shallots, finely sliced
250 g raw school prawns, heads removed, legs and tails trimmed to get rid of any sharp bits (do. not. peel. please. I beg of you.)
4 spring onions, cut into 3 cm batons
steamed rice, to serve (optional)

In a large bowl, combine the pork belly, fish sauce, sugar, garlic and pepper. You're gonna leave this to marinate for 15 minutes.

Heat the oil in a large frying pan or wok over high heat. Throw in the shallot and cook for 10 seconds, then add the pork belly, including the marinade. Cook for 2 minutes or until the pork is browned, then add the prawns and stir-fry for 2 minutes or until the prawns change colour. Finish by tossing through the spring onion and cooking for another minute. If you like, serve with rice.

TAMARIND CRAB

TIPS: ADD SOME COOKED THIN
EGG NOODS AT THE SAME TIME
AS THE TAMARIND MIXTURE IF
YOU NEED SOME CARBS TO SOAK UP
THE SAUCE.

I USUALLY LIKE TO DIP LONG THIN
CHINESE DOUGHNUTS INTO THE
SAUCE TO MOP IT ALL UP.

Move over chilli crab, there's a new player in town. If you've ever had the pleasure of visiting Vietnam and seeing the crowded tables along the side streets of Ho Chi Minh City, tamarind crab is probably what everyone was eating. In HCMC, this dish is made with swimmer crab, but we always had it with mud crab, due to how abundant they are in my parents' hometown of Ca Mau in Southern Vietnam. Ca Mau is inland and full of mangroves, making it great for mud-crabbing.

For me, fidgeting with the less-meaty swimmer crabs is much more rewarding and, because of the environment they live in, I find the flavours a little more complex (Mum always bagged me out for having a cheap palate because of how much more expensive the mud crabs were). If you would prefer a meatier dish feel free to use mud crabs in this recipe instead.

P.S. Don't be too scared of the chilli here, the long red ones add a lot of flavour and not too much heat!

SERVES 2

4 blue swimmer crabs
75 g (½ cup) tapioca starch
peanut oil, for deep-frying
1½ tablespoons tamarind pulp
3 tablespoons rice wine
3 tablespoons boiling water
2 tablespoons vegetable oil
4 garlic cloves, finely chopped
1 onion, cut into 6 wedges
6 spring onions, white parts only, cut into 5 cm lengths and halved
3 tablespoons fish sauce
2 long red chillies, halved lengthways
1 teaspoon ground white pepper

Begin by cleaning the crabs, removing the outer shells and gills and rinsing well. Reserve any crab mustard (this is the yellow–orangey stuff inside the shell). Cut the crab into quarters and gently break the claws using a pestle or the back of a meat cleaver.

Tip the tapioca starch into a bowl. Toss in the crab quarters to coat and shake off any excess starch.

Fill a large deep saucepan to about one-third full with peanut oil and heat to 180°C or until a cube of bread dropped in the oil browns in 15 seconds. Working in batches if necessary, deep-fry the crab pieces for 40–60 seconds, until the shells change colour to a bright orangey red. Carefully remove the crab and set aside to drain on paper towel.

In a small bowl, mix the tamarind pulp, rice wine and water and set aside.

Heat the vegetable oil in a large wok over high heat. Add the garlic and sauté for about 20 seconds until soft. Throw in the crab along with any reserved crab mustard and cook for 1–2 minutes, keeping everything moving with a spatula. Add the tamarind mixture and the remaining ingredients and cook for 2–4 minutes until the liquid has reduced by half.

Transfer the crab to a serving platter, pour the pan juices over the top, then get in and get your hands dirty.

CHICKEN NOODLE SOUP

PHO GA

Pho is the national dish of Vietnam and pho ga is the more neglected – and very seldom homemade – chicken version of the classic beef pho bo. Growing up, we never really had this at home since, in my mum's eyes, it wasn't worth making as it was so easy to get at numerous pho restaurants around our hometown of Springvale. While she's sort of right, just imagine how impressive it would be to say to your mates, 'Hey, come round for homemade pho.'

This light and delicious dish is perfect for a rainy Sunday dinner in the middle of winter or as a nourishing breakfast on any day of the week. It's that damn good. The aim here is to keep the broth as clear as possible, almost like a consomme, with the spices and herbs dancing delicately on your palate. My recipe calls for sriracha and hoisin sauces, which Mum would kill me for because it's not traditional, but I think it's so yummmmmm.

SERVES 4

2 small onions, unpeeled
1 piece of ginger, the size of two fingers, unpeeled
3 red shallots, unpeeled
1 tablespoon coriander seeds
3 cloves
2 star anise
1 cinnamon stick
1 free-range or walking chicken (see Tips; Asian butchers will know what a walking chicken is)
300 g daikon, peeled
2 tablespoons fish sauce
1½ tablespoons rock sugar (see Tips page 47)
2 teaspoons sea salt
½ bunch of coriander, leaves picked, stems and roots reserved

VINEGAR ONIONS
1 onion, finely sliced
250 ml (1 cup) white vinegar
1 tablespoon caster sugar

TO SERVE
500 g fresh flat rice noodles (cooked according to packet instructions)
270 g (3 cups) bean sprouts
1 bunch of Thai basil, leaves picked
½ bunch of coriander, leaves picked
sliced spring onion
sliced long red chilli
2 limes, halved
hoisin sauce
sriracha chilli sauce
pickled chilli (see Tips; optional)

Char the onions, ginger and shallots over an open flame until the skins are black. You can do this over burning coals (ideally) or on a gas barbecue or stovetop. Using a small knife, scrape off all the black burnt bits and discard (otherwise this will colour your broth). Place the onions, ginger and shallots in a 10 litre stockpot.

In a small dry frying pan over medium heat, toast the coriander seeds, cloves, star anise and cinnamon for 45–90 seconds until fragrant. Place the spices into a clean muslin cloth, wrap and tie tightly with kitchen string. Now chuck it in the stockpot.

Fill your kettle and bring to the boil. Place the whole chicken into your (clean!) sink and pour the boiling water over the top so it blanches the skin. This will keep the broth nice and clear by washing any impurities off the chicken.

Pop the chicken and daikon into the pot and cover with 5 litres of cold water. Bring to the boil over high heat, then reduce to a simmer and cook for 30 minutes. Use a ladle to skim any impurities that float to the top.

Add the fish sauce, sugar, salt and coriander stems and roots and cook for a further 15–20 minutes until the chicken is cooked through. You can test this by carefully removing the chicken from the pot, then piercing the thigh with a knife – if the juices run clear it's cooked.

Strain the broth into a clean saucepan and discard the solids.

Allow the chicken to cool then shred the meat and set aside for serving.

Meanwhile, to make the vinegar onions, place all the ingredients in a non-reactive bowl. Cover with 125 ml (½ cup) of water and leave to pickle for 30 minutes. Drain.

ADDICTED

TIPS: THE TRADITIONAL
CHICKEN USED FOR MAKING
PHO GA IS A 'WALKING
CHICKEN' (WE GREW UP
CALLING THEM THIS AND
I HAVE NO IDEA WHAT ELSE
THEY ARE CALLED). THESE
CHICKENS ARE LESS MEATY
AND ARE TALLER THAN THE
AVERAGE CHICKEN, AND HAVE
A SLIGHT YELLOW TINGE TO
THEIR SKIN. THESE BIRDS ARE
SWEETER AND HOLD MORE
FAT, WHICH MAKES THEM
PERFECT FOR PHO.

IF YOU CAN FIND A JAR OF
PICKLED CHILLI (SOMETIMES
SOLD AS PICKLED GROUND
CHILLI) AT YOUR LOCAL ASIAN
GROCER, BUY IT BECAUSE
YOU NEED TO HAVE IT ON
HAND AT ALL TIMES. A SMALL
TABLESPOON IN THIS SOUP
WILL MAKE IT THAT MUCH
MORE SPECIAL.

When you're ready to serve, heat the broth to a simmer over medium–high heat. Divide the noodles among four deep bowls and top with a nice handful of bean sprouts. Lay some shredded chicken in each bowl with a handful of basil and coriander leaves and some sliced spring onion. Ladle just enough broth into each bowl to cover the noodles and some of the chicken. Top with some of the vinegar onions and serve with chilli, lime halves, hoisin, sriracha and pickled chilli (if you like) on the side.

CHICKEN NOODLE
SOUP AKA PHO GA
(PAGES 52-3)

TO HOISIN, OR NOT
TO HOISIN, THAT
IS THE QUESTION

MUM'S SWEET and SOUR SQUID

MUC XAO THOM

Mum's sweet and sour squid is a favourite in our household. The sweet and succulent squid is accented by the acidity of the tomatoes and pineapple. To dial down the sour in the dish you can scoop out the seeds from the tomatoes, but I love this dish just the way it is. My uncle, who goes fishing regularly, would always bring over a freshly caught squid and I would watch Mum clean it from about 1 km away – I was too scared of getting squid juice on me. Now, I just get my fishmonger to deal with it.

SERVES 4

400 g squid (about 2 squid)
1 bird's eye chilli, chopped
2 tablespoons light soy sauce
1 tablespoon vegetable oil
3 garlic cloves, finely chopped
2 tomatoes, each cut into 6 wedges
1 Lebanese cucumber, halved
   lengthways, then cut into 4 cm
   pieces on the diagonal
200 g fresh pineapple, peeled and
   cut into 2 cm thick wedges
1 onion, cut into 6 wedges
2 tablespoons fish sauce
handful of Chinese celery leaves
   (see Tip), roughly chopped
2 sprigs of dill, roughly chopped
handful of coriander leaves
pinch of sea salt
1 teaspoon ground white pepper
steamed rice, to serve (optional)

Begin by cleaning the squid. Rinse thoroughly, then remove and discard the head and quill. Cut the tube of the squid open then slice into pieces about as thick as your thumb. Cut the tentacles into 5 cm pieces and set aside.

Stir the chopped chilli into the soy sauce to make a dipping sauce.

Heat the vegetable oil in a wok over high heat. Add the garlic and cook for 20–30 seconds until fragrant. Add the squid and cook, stirring to coat it in the garlic, for 1–2 minutes until the squid begins to change colour.

Add the tomato, cucumber, pineapple, onion and fish sauce. Turn the heat down to medium and cook for 2–3 minutes until the tomato starts to break down and soften. Add the Chinese celery, mix well and cover for 2 minutes.

Stir through the dill, coriander, salt and pepper, then spoon everything onto a serving plate. Serve with rice, if you like, and with the dipping sauce on the side.

TIP: CHINESE CELERY IS AVAILABLE FROM ASIAN GROCERS. WHEN I CAN'T FIND IT, I SUBSTITUTE WITH LOVAGE OR THE LEAVES FROM THE TOP OF REGULAR CELERY, AS THE FLAVOUR IS QUITE SIMILAR.

LEMONGRASS and SAKE CLAMS

NGHEU HAP SA

Ask any Vietnamese person about ngheu hap sa (lemongrass clams) and you'll see their face light up with excitement. This dish, usually served in shellfish cafes in hems (alleyways) around Vietnam as the sun tucks itself to bed, is fantastically fragrant and so moreish. Sweet and salty from the clams themselves with zing and floral notes from the lemongrass, the hum from the ginger and chilli should be just enough to give the dish warmth but not too much heat. The chillies are kept whole so they infuse flavour without blowing your head off, although I have been known to eat them straight from the broth.

My take on this dish adds citrus flavour through the use of makrut lime leaves (see page 13) and sweetness from sake (inspired by a version made with rice wine I ate when I was on the Mekong Delta with my little sister). Funnily enough, this dish is one my mum makes to bribe me to come home when it's been too many weeks between visits.

SERVES 2

2 bird's eye chillies
75 ml sake
2.5 cm piece of ginger, lightly smashed
2 lemongrass stalks, white part only, lightly smashed and chopped into 5 cm lengths
2 tablespoons crushed garlic
1 teaspoon caster sugar
1 kg fresh baby clams or pipis

TO SERVE

2.5 cm piece of ginger, finely chopped
1 lemongrass stalk, white part only, finely chopped
handful of coriander leaves
3 makrut lime leaves (see page 13), finely sliced
chopped bird's eye chilli (optional)
freshly ground black pepper (optional)

Place the chillies, sake, ginger, lemongrass, garlic and sugar in a wide shallow saucepan with a lid over high heat and add 300 ml of water. Once the liquid comes to the boil, add the clams, cover to steam and infuse for 3 minutes. When the clams open they'll release the beautiful salty juices from inside their shells. Remove the clams as they open (discarding any that don't) and transfer to a serving bowl with some pieces of the cooked lemongrass.

Pour the hot clam broth into the serving dish, then scatter with the finely chopped ginger and lemongrass, coriander and makrut lime.

If you like it hot, feel free to add chopped fresh chilli and a nice crack of black pepper.

TIP: IF YOU WANT TO MAKE THIS A MORE SUBSTANTIAL MAIN DISH, IT GOES REALLY WELL WITH VERMICELLI NOODLES. POP 80 G OF DRIED VERMICELLI NOODLES PER PERSON INTO THE LIQUID JUST BEFORE ADDING THE CLAMS. THEY WILL TAKE ROUGHLY THE SAME TIME TO COOK AND WILL SOAK UP THE WONDERFUL FLAVOURS.

HUE-STYLE BEEF NOODLE SOUP

BUN BO HUE

Bun bo Hue is hands down my favourite Vietnamese noodle dish, which is why it was my signature dish on *MasterChef Australia* 2020, although this recipe is more traditional than the version I did on the show. While it's not as well known here, bun bo Hue is one of the most commonly eaten dishes throughout Vietnam, where you'll find a vendor on practically every street corner. The spice is mouth watering – a little tangy from the pineapple and the beef bones make it extra rich. I remember begging my mum to make me this soup growing up, not knowing how much care and love the dish needed to really let the flavours develop. This is not a recipe for a quick Monday dinner, this is defs a Saturday/Sunday arvo, post-market visit love affair. Give it time, attention and adore it while you cook and I'm sure it will become a family favourite of yours, too.

SERVES 8

400 g thick dried rice noodles
1 fresh banana blossom (see Tips), outer leaves and bud discarded, petals washed and finely shredded
¼ red cabbage, finely shredded
400 g water spinach, cut into thirds
400 g bean sprouts
1 bunch of Vietnamese mint, leaves picked
½ bunch of mint, leaves picked
½ bunch of coriander, leaves picked
½ bunch of Thai basil, leaves picked
3 spring onions, green parts only, finely sliced

SPICED OIL

125 ml (½ cup) neutral oil (such as vegetable or grapeseed)
1 tablespoon annatto seeds (see Tips)
2 lemongrass stalks, white part only, finely chopped
2 red shallots, finely chopped
5 cm piece of ginger, finely chopped
1 long red chilli, finely chopped
1½ tablespoons fermented shrimp paste (mam ruoc Hue, see Tips)
2 teaspoons chilli powder
1 tablespoon onion powder
3 teaspoons ground ginger

To make the spiced oil, place the oil and annatto seeds in a small frying pan over medium heat. Bring to a simmer and cook for 5–7 minutes until the annatto seeds release an orange–red colour into the oil. Strain, reserving the oil and discarding the seeds. Return the oil to the frying pan over medium heat and bring to 160°C or until a cube of bread dropped in the oil browns in 25 seconds. Add the lemongrass, shallot, ginger and chilli and cook for 2–3 minutes until fragrant. Add the shrimp paste and cook, stirring, for 1 minute. Add the chilli powder, onion powder and ground ginger and cook for another minute – you want everything to incorporate but not burn. Set aside.

To make the broth, place the bones, trotter, oxtail, gravy beef and brisket into a 15 litre stockpot. Cover with cold water, add 2 tablespoons of salt and bring to the boil over high heat. Cook for 10 minutes at a rolling boil. Tip into a large colander, draining the liquid, then rinse the bones and meat in warm water to wash away any impurities.

Clean the stockpot and return the meat and bones to the pot along with the lemongrass, onion, pineapple, ginger, sugar, stock cubes and 8 litres of cold water (if this doesn't cover your bones then just add more). Add the spiced oil and bring to the boil over high heat. Turn the heat to low and simmer for 2 hours, skimming any impurities that rise to the surface every 20 minutes or so. Remove the gravy beef and brisket and set aside in the fridge. Add the fish sauce and 2 teaspoons of salt to the broth and simmer for a further 1 hour. (Don't strain the broth because you want the wonderful aromatics in the oil to be served in your dish.)

FLAVOUR BOMB!

BROTH

1 kg beef bones, cut into fist-sized chunks (ask your butcher to do this)

1 beef marrow bone, cut into quarters (ask your butcher to do this)

400 g pig's trotters, cut into eighths (your butcher will do this, too)

500 g oxtail

500 g gravy beef (boneless beef shank)

500 g brisket beef

sea salt

3 lemongrass stalks, white parts only, bruised with the back of a knife

1 onion, peeled and quartered

1 pineapple, peeled and cut into 8 pieces

10 cm piece of ginger, peeled and quartered

5 cm piece of yellow rock sugar (see Tips page 47)

3 beef stock cubes

3 tablespoons fish sauce

When you're ready to serve, cook the rice noodles according to the packet instructions and divide among eight large serving bowls. Finely slice the gravy beef and brisket and divide into the bowls. Top with the banana blossom, cabbage, water spinach, bean sprouts and herbs. Ladle 400–500 ml (depending on the bowl size) of broth over the top – the broth should have a nice amount oil floating on top – and finish with a sprinkling of spring onion.

TIPS: BANANA BLOSSOMS ARE AVAILABLE AT ASIAN GROCERS. DON'T BOTHER WITH THE CANNED VARIETY AS THE PURPOSE IS TO ADD CRUNCH. IF YOU CAN'T FIND IT FRESH, JUST LEAVE IT OUT.

ANNATTO SEEDS ARE SMALL AND RED WITH A POWDERY COATING. THEY HAVE AN EARTHY AND PEPPERY FLAVOUR AND ARE AVAILABLE FROM ASIAN GROCERS.

MAM RUOC HUE IS FERMENTED SHRIMP PASTE, THOUGH IT'S SOMETIMES ALSO MADE WITH FERMENTED ANCHOVIES. NOT TO BE MISTAKEN FOR THE MORE COMMONLY AVAILABLE MALAYSIAN SHRIMP PASTE (BELACHAN), MAM RUOC HUE IS USUALLY A PURPLEISH COLOUR AND HAS A VERY STRONG SMELL.

CHAPTER TWO

THE FAMILY WE CHOOSE

COOKING FOR (AND WITH!) YOUR FRIENDS

Without my friends, I would be an absolute bubbling mess. They give me advice on boys, career and fashion; they make me laugh and cry and laugh again. They cut me down when I'm being arrogant and build me up when I question every single decision I've ever made. Sometimes they tell me what I want to hear, sometimes they tell me what I don't want to hear, but they are always there when I need someone to just listen. They say things like 'you are strong, you can do better than him, he was a drainer, now you can DM cute 6 am gym guy' or 'you look dumb, why are you wearing leather slides to pilates?'.

I couldn't survive without my friends. First there are my gays, who I regularly use as guinea pigs for new dishes. I like to cook when I'm hungover – it's kinda my thing – so it's just expected now that if I drink with them on Friday night, then Saturday lunch I'll be cooking for them.

My old friends who have been there for over a decade. They were there when I was having packaged taco nights in a studio apartment and they are still here now when I make cheese platters that have exotic, high-altitude Swiss gruyeres. (I know it sounds wanky but it's the bomb – really sharp, hard and with extra spicy notes. The Cheese Room at Emerald Deli in South Melbourne Market will hook you up – ask for Maria or scream her name and greet her with a hug like I do, I think she likes that ... or she might just be too nice to tell me to piss off.)

My new friends, who are lovely enough to share their special recipes with me. I'm so thankful for this because it's not always about how long you've known someone for. Friendships can be important and meaningful in so many different ways.

My housemate, Diana, who has separation anxiety (one time I got up from the couch to get water and she actually panicked and screamed 'WHERE ARE YOU GOING?!' ... Ummm, for water you psychopath). Anyway, I love her for it. We also throw hissy fits together when our food is under seasoned.

This chapter is full of recipes to share, to spill tea over or enjoy with a bottle of wine. There are recipes you can make for a long lunch or dinner party. Recipes you can eat while you have Bumble connected to the TV so that you can swipe as a group (yes, we do this). Recipes you can cook with your #girlgang.

People say they get worried about cooking for me, but I feel like when someone cooks for you, feeds you, nourishes you, they are doing it out of love, so to me that is always appreciated. Try these recipes, spend some time over good food with your people – you'll love each other more for it.

WHAT'S IN THIS CHAPTER?

♡ DISHES THAT WILL HAVE YOU SORTED FOR A POTLUCK DINNER. TRY MY RAGU FOR YOU (PAGE 86) OR CHEESEBURGER SPRING ROLLS (PAGE 68).

♡ OLD CROWD PLEASERS THAT NOW HAVE A NEW TWIST, LIKE SAUSAGE ROLLS (PAGE 72) AND SPAG BOL (PAGE 78).

♡ DESSERTS THAT WE ALL PRETEND WE DON'T NEED BUT SOMEHOW END UP DISAPPEARING THROUGHOUT THE NIGHT.

♡ THE PERFECT ADDITION TO A CHEESE BOARD FOR YOU TO GOSSIP OVER (PAGE 66). (SORRY, WHO ARE WE TALKING ABOUT? I WASN'T PAYING ATTENTION, THE BRIE WAS TALKING TO ME ...)

BAKED BRIE *with* ROSEMARY *and* FIGS

Baked brie isn't new but it's always impressive as a centrepiece for a cheese platter. It's so easy and I can guarantee it will be a winner at your next dinner party or catch-up over a bottle of rosé. This is one of those dishes that I whip out when I'm cooking dinner and it's taking longer than expected. I serve it with some crackers, nuts and crudités to keep my guests distracted and chatting while I quietly freak out over how long dinner is taking to finish. It's also really good to take to a barbecue – skip the figs, then you can just prepare it and pop it in the oven for 16–20 minutes when you arrive!

Warning: baked brie addiction is a real thing, so be careful.

SERVES 4

200 g wheel of good-quality brie
2 rosemary sprigs, roughly torn
2 garlic cloves, sliced
2 tablespoons honey
2 figs, each cut into 6 pieces
sturdy crackers, crusty bread or crudités, such as carrots and celery, to serve

Preheat the oven to 180°C.

Place the brie in an ovenproof dish that's just big enough to hold it snugly. Score the top of the cheese in two directions so that the cuts make diamond shapes, cutting about halfway down. Stick the rosemary and garlic into the cuts.

Pop the brie in the oven for 10 minutes. Pull it out and spoon 1 tablespoon of honey over the top. Scatter the figs onto the cheese, then drizzle with the remaining honey. Pop it back in the oven for another 8–12 minutes until the honey starts to caramelise and the figs have softened.

Remove from the oven and get in there while it's warm and gooey. Serve with your favourite crackers, some crusty bread or crudités to dip into that oozy cheese.

CHEESEBURGER SPRING ROLLS

Cheeseburgers, the second national dish of Vietnam! Okay, I'm lying, but seriously, who doesn't love cheeseburgers? These spring rolls came about when I was preparing for a cooking demonstration and racking my brain to come up with something that was delicious and fun. What I came up with was something salivatingly sinful. The secret to this truly tasting like a cheeseburger is in the dipping sauce – be warned though, because that sauce pretty much goes on everything I eat now. These crispy little parcels of heaven, perfect as a canapé, are a major hit with all my mates.

Side note: these have been known to win over even the coldest of hearts.

MAKES 24

2 eggs
1 teaspoon olive oil
150 g beef mince (the higher the fat content, the better)
100 g pork mince
¼ red onion, diced
1 tablespoon chopped flat-leaf parsley leaves
1 teaspoon garlic powder
½ teaspoon freshly ground black pepper
1 tablespoon seeded mustard
35 g (¼ cup) grated mozzarella
25 g (¼ cup) dried breadcrumbs
2 tablespoons chopped chives
1 garlic clove, crushed
1 tablespoon Worcestershire sauce
pinch of sea salt
24 spring roll wrappers
neutral oil for deep-frying (such as vegetable oil)

SECRET DIPPING SAUCE

125 ml (½ cup) kewpie mayo
1 tablespoon tomato sauce
2 teaspoons finely chopped dill pickle
1 teaspoon yellow American mustard
¼ teaspoon smoked paprika

Lightly whisk one of the eggs in a large bowl, add all the remaining ingredients except the wrappers and oil and mix well.

In a small bowl, beat the remaining egg – you'll use this to bind the wrapped spring rolls.

Place a spring roll wrapper on a clean work surface with a corner pointing towards you. Keep the remaining wrappers covered while you work so they don't dry out. Spread a heaped tablespoon of the mixture about two-thirds the length of the wrapper in a thick line. Fold the sides of the wrapper in towards the centre. Brush the wrapper with the egg wash and, starting with the corner closest to you, roll up to make a spring roll. Repeat with the remaining wrappers and mixture. You should end up with 24 spring rolls.

Meanwhile, to make the secret dipping sauce, mix all the ingredients in a small bowl.

Fill a small saucepan to about one-third full with oil and heat to 180°C or until a cube of bread dropped in the oil browns in 15 seconds.

Working in batches of three or four (you don't want to overcrowd the pan), fry the spring rolls for 4–6 minutes, turning occasionally, until golden and crisp. Carefully remove and drain on paper towel.

Serve hot with the secret dipping sauce.

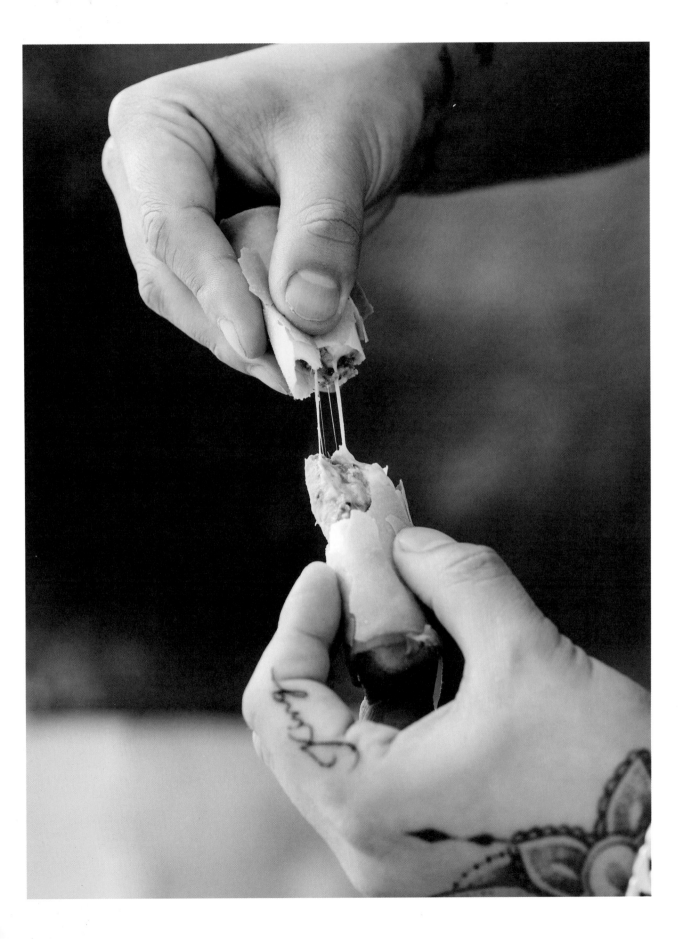

THESE CRISPY PARCELS HAVE BEEN KNOWN TO WIN OVER EVEN THE COLDEST OF HEARTS.

PORK, GINGER and LIME SAUSAGE ROLLS

You know when you're asked to bring a dish to your partner's family dinner or friend's gathering/barbecue/drinks or nephew's home viola concert. (Yes, apparently it's a thing.) This is the perfect dish for those occasions – an absolute showstopper and crowd pleaser. The aromatic lime leaf and ginger really sing in these flaky sausage rolls, which have a wonderful sweetness from the pork and onion.

MAKES 48

3 sheets puff pastry, defrosted and cut in half
1 egg, lightly beaten with a little water
sesame seeds, for sprinkling

SAUSAGE FILLING
500 g pork mince (the higher the fat content, the better)
60 g (⅓ cup) grated onion, juice squeezed out
50 g (⅓ cup) grated carrot
1 egg, lightly beaten
30 g (½ cup) panko breadcrumbs
2 spring onions, finely chopped
handful of coriander leaves, finely chopped
2 teaspoons grated ginger
2 tablespoons finely chopped makrut lime leaves (see page 13)
2 teaspoons sriracha chilli sauce
1 teaspoon light soy sauce
2 teaspoons fish sauce
zest and juice of ½ lime
½ teaspoon sea salt
1 teaspoon garlic powder
1 teaspoon ground white pepper

Preheat the oven to 210°C. Line two baking trays with baking paper.

To make the filling, place all the ingredients in a large bowl and give it a really good mix to make sure everything's well combined.

Place a rectangle of puff pastry on a clean work surface. Spoon about one-sixth of the filling close to the long edge of the pastry and shape it into a log. Brush the edge of the pastry with egg wash, then carefully roll it up tightly and seal.

Brush the top of the sausage roll with the egg wash and sprinkle with sesame seeds. Cut into 8 even-sized pieces and place on one of the prepared baking trays. Repeat the process with the remaining pastry and filling to make 48 sausage rolls.

Bake for 25–30 minutes or until puffed and golden.

TIP: THE OBVIOUS SAUCE CHOICE FOR THESE IS SWEET CHILLI, BUT TOMATO SAUCE GOES REALLY WELL WITH THEM, TOO. I ALSO LIKE TO SERVE THEM WITH SOY SAUCE THAT HAS HAD FRESH RED CHILLIES CUT INTO IT USING A PAIR OF KITCHEN SCISSORS (THAT'S DEFS THE VIET IN ME).

FURIKAKE OMELETTE RICE

One of my best friends and I had this thing about not knowing how to cook rice, so we spent a day learning together. It's actually a very sad way to spend your day, but we came out of it with this dish so I defs don't regret it. It may not seem like much, but this dish is an absolute umami bomb, a powerhouse of flavour.

P.S. I always make extra dashi so that I have some in my freezer ready to go. It's very convenient to have on hand and adds so much flavour to many dishes.

SERVES 2

200 g (1 cup) jasmine rice
4 eggs
2 teaspoons light soy sauce
2 teaspoons mirin
2 teaspoons cooking sake
pinch of sea salt
1 tablespoon neutral oil (such as vegetable oil)
½ onion, finely sliced into half moons
2 tablespoons furikake (see Tip)
small handful of chives, finely chopped

DASHI:
10 cm square piece of kombu
10 g (1 cup) dried bonito flakes

TIP: FURIKAKE IS A JAPANESE SEASONING (TRADITIONALLY SPRINKLED ON RICE). IT USUALLY CONTAINS DRIED FISH, SESAME SEEDS, SEAWEED AND SPICES FOR AN INTENSE UMAMI HIT. IT'S AVAILABLE FROM ASIAN GROCERS.

To make the dashi, place the kombu and 1 litre (4 cups) of water in a saucepan over high heat and bring to the boil. Simmer for 10 minutes, skimming any impurities that rise to the top. Remove and discard the kombu. Stir in the bonito flakes and simmer for 5 minutes. Turn off the heat, leave to infuse for 10 minutes, then strain, reserving the liquid. This will make about 600–700 ml of dashi – you won't need all of it for this recipe. Leftovers will keep in the fridge for up to 1 week or in the freezer for up to 1 month.

Place the rice in a small saucepan with 375 ml (1½ cups) of the dashi and place over high heat. Cover with a lid and bring to the boil (this should take 3–5 minutes). Reduce the heat to low and simmer, covered, for 8–10 minutes until the liquid is absorbed. Turn off the heat and leave, covered, for another 10 minutes, then fluff with a fork and set aside.

In a bowl, whisk the eggs, soy, mirin, sake and salt and set aside.

Heat half the oil in a large wok over high heat, add half the onion and cook, stirring, for about 5 minutes until softened. Pour in half the egg mixture, reduce the heat to medium and cook for about 5 minutes, using a silicone spatula to pull the cooked edge of the egg mixture in towards the centre of the wok every 30 seconds or so, until all the egg is cooked. Remove, set aside and repeat with the remaining oil, onion and egg mixture.

Divide the rice between two shallow bowls and place the omelettes on top of the rice. Sprinkle the furikake and chives over the top of the omelettes and serve.

DHAL PASTA for MY DARLS

A little while ago I had a dinner planned with a group of mates that included two people who eat a plant-based diet and my bestie, Tara, who is coeliac. This basically sent me spiralling into my own little *MasterChef* challenge. I was at the supermarket, looking through all the different pastas and saw a red lentil pasta that Tara had recommended. I also remembered obsessing over her delicious dhal recipe and that's how this dish was born. It made total sense in my mind: red lentils are used to make dhal so I can just use the dahl as a sauce for my red lentil pasta. Italian–Indian, I think that's officially a thing now. This dish is comforting, very familiar but also very new and exciting on the palate because you don't expect the spices when you first see the pasta.

SERVES 2 HUNGRY PEOPLE

1 teaspoon coconut oil
1 large onion, finely diced
1 teaspoon cumin seeds
1 teaspoon coriander seeds
1 teaspoon mustard seeds
3 teaspoons ground turmeric
1½ teaspoons garam masala
4 garlic cloves, crushed
1 tablespoon grated ginger
1 long red chilli, finely chopped
200 g red lentils, rinsed and drained
400 ml passata
400 ml can coconut milk
400 ml vegetable stock
sea salt and freshly ground
  black pepper
250 g red lentil pasta (if you're not
  GF then you can use regular pasta
  if you want)
juice of 1 lemon
2 packed cups shredded
  cavolo nero

Melt the coconut oil in a saucepan over medium heat, add the onion and cook for 6–8 minutes until softened.

Meanwhile, toast the cumin, coriander and mustard seeds in a dry frying pan over medium heat, stirring, for 1–2 minutes until the mustard seeds pop. Place in a spice grinder with the turmeric and garam masala, grind to a fine powder and set aside.

Add the garlic, ginger and chilli to the onion and cook for 2 minutes, then pop the ground spices in and cook, stirring, for a further minute.

Add the lentils, passata, coconut milk and stock and reduce the heat to medium–low. Simmer for 20 minutes until nice and thick, stirring occasionally to make sure it doesn't catch and burn.

While the lentils are cooking, bring a large saucepan of heavily salted water to the boil. Cook the pasta according to the packet instructions (I like to cook mine for 1–1½ minutes less for that al dente bite). Drain.

Season the lentils with salt, pepper and lemon juice and stir through the cavolo nero until it wilts. Add the cooked pasta and mix well. Dish it up and let everyone get confused by the mix of spices and pasta. (Is this Indian pasta ...? Yes.)

MOST YUMMY THING?

- The first piece of pasta you eat as a tester to see if it's cooked
- The fruit your mum randomly brings you
- Popcorn as you're walking into a movie
- The cheeseboard you gossip over
- The piece of leftover ham that you have three hours after your food coma on Christmas Day
- Even the worst fish and chips if it's by the ocean
- The seventh vodka, lime and soda you have on a night out when the conversation is amazing
- Any takeaway your partner brings home after a long day
- The cookie you eat before waiting for it to cool down
- Men that are so wrong for you.

OOH YES!

MY SPAG BOL

After one of our busiest night of service at @thegeorgeoncollins, I was lying in bed thinking about how I was craving pasta – my favourite pasta – a dish that reminded me why I fell in love with food. Because food should be joyous, bringing up memories and emotions.

Spag bol, as I've always called it, reminds me of cooking as a child. Mum never made spag bol for me, purely because it wasn't part of her repertoire, so it was one of the first things I ever cooked for her. I didn't really know what I was doing at the time (I garnished it with coriander ... tragic!).

So, back to that night – I went to bed seriously craving spag bol and sent out a cheeky message to some friends that read, 'Hey, if you're not busy, I'll be going to the market after the gym tomorrow to grab ingredients to make a slow spag bol from scratch, come over for a late lunch.'

The next day, I spent the morning at the Prahran Market picking up some wonderful ingredients from my favourite @pinosfineproduce to make a 2½-hour spag bol. Cooking a dish loved by so many made me happy, sharing it with my friends made me happy, spending time gently simmering a sauce so everything infused made me happy and making something that brought back memories made me happy.

I want to share all that with you, so please give my spag bol recipe a try. The anchovies add a wonderful hint of funk to the dish, the milk and wine add body and complexity, and I season with Vegemite, which gives it an umami kick and the richness that the dish craves. This dish is slow but it's worth it, so make it for your loved ones, share it with your friends and family.

SERVES 6

2 tablespoons extra-virgin olive oil
60 g butter
1 onion, finely chopped
2 large carrots, finely chopped
3 celery stalks, finely chopped
4 garlic cloves, crushed
1 bunch of basil, leaves picked and stems finely chopped
6 anchovy fillets
200 g pancetta, diced
500 g beef mince
500 g pork mince
1 teaspoon dried oregano
3 dried bay leaves
½ teaspoon fresh thyme leaves
2 x 400 g cans diced tomatoes
1 litre (4 cups) good-quality beef stock
250 ml (1 cup) red wine
250 ml (1 cup) full-cream milk
1 teaspoon Vegemite
sea salt and freshly ground black pepper
500–700 g thick spaghetti (or your favourite pasta)
grated Parmigiano Reggiano, to serve

Heat the oil and butter in a large heavy-based saucepan over medium heat until the butter has melted (the oil stops the butter from burning). Add the onion, carrot and celery and cook for about 10 minutes until softened. Add the garlic, basil stems, anchovy fillets and pancetta and cook for 6–8 minutes until the pancetta takes on some colour.

Add the beef and pork mince and cook, using a wooden spoon to break up the mince, for 6–8 minutes until browned. Add the oregano, bay leaves, thyme and tomatoes and cook for 5 minutes.

Pour the stock into the tomato cans to rinse all the tomatoey goodness before adding to the pan. Add the wine, reduce the heat to a simmer and cook for 1–1½ hours.

Add the milk, stir well, then add the Vegemite. Simmer for another 30 minutes, then season with salt and pepper.

When ready to serve, bring a large saucepan of heavily salted water to the boil. Add the spaghetti and cook for 2 minutes less than the packet instructions. Don't drain your pasta, but grab a pair of tongs and lift your pasta straight out of the pan and plonk it into the sauce. This way you don't lose too much liquid and the starchy water helps to make the sauce even better.

Divide the spag bol among serving plates and top with a generous amount of grated Parmigiano Reggiano.

NEEDS MORE CHEESE!

MY SPAG BOL (PAGE 78)

GNOCCHI for GAYS

Gnocchi for gays. I made this recipe because I was way overdue for a catch-up with my favourite boys – one of whom is actually holding this dish in the photo on the next page ... nice arms, right? I served this alongside three salads and two other pasta dishes, but I think we all agreed that this was the absolute stand-out of the day, which is why it's here for you.

Let's talk about my gays. They make me laugh, they make me cry, they deal with my melodramatic and melancholic personality, they make me want abs (they all have abs; I don't know how that's even possible due to their constant consumption of carbs). They sometimes make me cringe, but without them I would be a sheltered gay man not fully exposed to our wonderful community. For that, I love them dearly.

SERVES 4–6 (OF MY FAVOURITE GAYS)

1 kg starchy potatoes, such as yukon gold or royal blue (try to choose potatoes that are medium sized and fairly uniform)
120–150 g plain flour, plus extra for dusting
sea salt
180 g butter, cut into cubes
1 bunch of sage, leaves picked
zest of 1 lemon
juice of ½ lemon
50 g (⅓ cup) toasted pine nuts
nice chunk of parmesan, to serve

Preheat the oven to 200°C.

Pop the potatoes on a baking tray and bake them for 35–45 minutes until you can prick them with a skewer with no resistance. Keep checking them because the time will depend on your spuds.

While the potatoes are still as hot as you can handle, chop them in half and use a spoon to scoop the insides into a mixing bowl. Using a potato ricer, rice the potato onto a lightly floured work surface.

Sift 120 g of the flour onto the potato and add a generous pinch of salt. Gently bring the potato and flour together into a dough. You don't want to overwork it, the dough should be soft and just holding together. If the mixture is too wet, add a little more flour. (You can test a pinch of dough by dropping it in boiling water – if it breaks apart, add more flour.)

Lightly flour your work surface again. Roll pieces of your perfect dough into logs about 2 cm thick, then cut into 3 cm lengths. You can roll each gnocchi over a fork if you're pairing them with a heartier sauce, but we are frying these so I like them to look like pillows.

Bring a large saucepan of heavily salted water to the boil and cook the gnocchi for 1–2 minutes until they rise to the surface.

While the gnocchi is cooking, pop 50 g of the butter in a large frying pan over medium heat. By the time the butter melts, your gnocchi should be starting to rise to the surface. As they do, lift them out with a slotted spoon, drain well, then throw them into the frying pan and cook, giving them a gentle toss occasionally to coat in the butter, for 2–4 minutes until golden. Transfer to a serving platter and keep warm.

Wipe out the frying pan, then throw in the remaining butter and cook over medium–high heat for 3–5 minutes or until brown and fragrant. Add the sage leaves and cook until crisp. Pour the sage butter over the gnocchi and sprinkle with the lemon zest and juice and toasted pine nuts.

Serve immediately with a block of parmesan and a cheese shaver, and let your mates add as much as they want.

PORK and FENNEL RAGU for YOU

You know what's really good? A big pot of pasta among friends. This dish always reminds me of a particular moment: a girlfriend of mine was six-months single, ready to get back on the dating scene but from a safe distance. So I had a group of friends over for some pasta on a rainy night and we signed her up to a dating app. That lasted all of 10 minutes, but this recipe? This recipe is a keeper. It's fragrant and filling, and gives you that carb hit we all sometimes need. Making this pasta always reminds me of that day – hopefully you can make it for your besties and create memories of your own. A great support system is the best thing you can have and maintaining one is not about big fancy dinners or elaborate brunches. Sometimes, it's as simple as a night with your nearest and dearest, flicking through dating apps with your phone connected to your TV, laughing over a bowl of pasta.

SERVES 4–8 (DEPENDING ON HOW HUNGRY YOU AND YOUR MATES ARE!)

3 tablespoons extra-virgin olive oil
600 g pork and fennel sausages, casings cut open and filling broken into bite-sized pieces
2 celery stalks, finely diced
1 large carrot, finely diced
1 onion, finely diced
2 teaspoons finely chopped sage leaves
4 garlic cloves, finely chopped
1 long red chilli, finely chopped (optional)
250 ml (1 cup) dry white wine
250 ml (1 cup) salt-reduced chicken stock
sea salt
600 g dried casarecce or any other pasta that you like
as much parmesan as you want (because why not?), to serve
chopped flat-leaf parsley leaves (as much as you can handle), to serve

Heat 1 tablespoon of the oil in a large saucepan over high heat. Add the sausage pieces and cook, turning, for about 5 minutes until browned. Remove from the pan and set aside.

Reduce the heat to medium and add the remaining oil to the pan along with the celery, carrot and onion. Cook for 5–7 minutes until the veggies have softened. Add the sage, garlic and chilli (if using) and cook for another 2 minutes.

Add the sausage pieces back in, along with the white wine and cook over high heat for 6–8 minutes until the liquid has almost completely evaporated. Add the chicken stock and cook for 10 minutes until a thick sauce forms (you don't want it to be watery). Season with salt (it should be a little bit salty, which will be balanced out by the pasta).

Meanwhile, bring a large saucepan of heavily salted water to the boil. Cook the pasta for 1–2 minutes less than the packet instructions, then drain, reserving about 250 ml (1 cup) of the cooking water. Tip the drained pasta into the sauce, along with some of the reserved water if you need to loosen the sauce. Cook for 1 minute, mixing well.

Spoon the pasta into serving bowls and top with heaps of parmesan and parsley. (Usually I serve myself a smaller portion and pretend I won't go back for more, but I always do ... lol.)

MALAYSIAN BEEF RENDANG

Back when we first moved in together, my housemate Diana Chan had a pop-up restaurant called Chanteen. I would beg her every week to bring home her rendang because it was defs my favourite dish on her menu and she would never give me the recipe. It's now a couple of years on and she still won't actually give me her real rendang recipe, but instead shared this shortcut version. Apparently, she's taking her other recipe to the grave (so selfish). This is still sooooo good and very close to what she would bring home for me – not too spicy and a little bit sweet.

SERVES 6

125 ml (½ cup) melted coconut oil or vegetable oil
1.5 kg chuck steak, gravy beef or brisket, cut into bite-sized pieces
500 ml (2 cups) canned coconut milk
3 tablespoons Malaysian curry powder (see Tips)
90 g (1 cup) desiccated coconut
3 tablespoons karamel masakan (see Tips)
sea salt
6 makrut lime leaves (see page 13), finely sliced
steamed rice, to serve

SPICE PASTE

6 dried red chillies, soaked in warm water for 15 minutes, then drained
2 lemongrass stalks, white parts roughly chopped, tops bruised and reserved
8 makrut lime leaves (see page 13), finely sliced
3 cm piece of fresh turmeric, roughly chopped or 2 teaspoons ground turmeric
5 cm piece of galangal, roughly chopped
6 red shallots, roughly chopped
5 garlic cloves, roughly chopped
4 long red chillies, roughly chopped
1 tablespoon vegetable oil

To make the spice paste, place all the ingredients except the vegetable oil in a food processor or blender and whiz into a fine paste. Pour the vegetable oil into a large saucepan over medium–low heat and saute the spice paste for 4–6 minutes until fragrant and the oil splits from the paste.

In a large frying pan over high heat, place the coconut oil and beef and brown for about 8 minutes, turning often to get good caramelisation all over. Transfer the beef to the saucepan with the spice paste.

Add the coconut milk, curry powder and reserved lemongrass tops and simmer for 3–3½ hours until the beef is tender and the liquid has reduced by half. Give it a stir every now and again and add some water if it starts looking a bit dry.

Meanwhile, toast the desiccated coconut in a dry frying pan over low heat for 5–7 minutes until golden brown. Add it to the pan with the beef and stir. Continue cooking for another 10 minutes, then stir through the karamel masakan and salt to taste. Finish with the lime leaves and serve over steamed rice.

TIPS: MALAYSIAN CURRY POWDER IS AVAILABLE FROM ASIAN GROCERS AND IS A BLEND OF TURMERIC, CORIANDER SEEDS, CHILLI, CUMIN, FENNEL, CINNAMON, WHITE PEPPER, BLACK PEPPER, CARDAMOM, STAR ANISE, NUTMEG, BAY LEAVES AND CLOVES.

KARAMEL MASAKAN IS A COOKING CARAMEL. IT IS AVAILABLE FROM ASIAN GROCERS AND SOME SUPERMARKETS. IF YOU CAN'T FIND IT, YOU CAN SUBSTITUTE KECAP MANIS.

BANANA FRITTERS

CHUOI CHIEN

Chuoi chien can be made using a mixture of plain and rice flour, with the addition of sesame seeds or even shredded coconut. My recipe takes it back to its purest form and is also gluten free. The addition of turmeric is for colour and earthiness to cut through the sweetness. You can also serve these with coconut caramel or honey. Yum!

SERVES 4

8 very ripe lady finger bananas, peeled (see Tip)
175 g (1 cup) rice flour, sifted
3 tablespoons cornflour
2 tablespoons caster sugar
½ teaspoon ground turmeric
¼ teaspoon sea salt
1 large egg
neutral oil for deep-frying (such as vegetable oil)

TO SERVE
icing sugar
warmed coconut cream
chopped roasted peanuts

TIP: FOR THE BANANAS, YOU WANT THEM TO BE VERY RIPE. I'M TALKING 'HALF A DAY BEFORE THEY'RE READY FOR BANANA BREAD' KIND OF RIPE. LADY FINGER BANANAS ARE PERFECT FOR FRITTERS BECAUSE YOU WANT A HIGH SUGAR CONTENT, BUT IF THEY'RE NOT AVAILABLE, USE FOUR BANANAS CUT IN HALF CROSSWAYS TO MAKE THEM SHORTER.

Place the bananas between two sheets of baking paper, making sure you leave plenty of space between each banana (you may need to do this in batches) and place a large heavy chopping board on top. Gently lean your weight on the chopping board until the bananas are squashed to 1 cm in thickness – don't go too hard, you want them to squish down without breaking apart. To help keep everything together, I pop the bananas in the freezer for an hour, just to firm up – you don't want to actually freeze them.

Meanwhile, in a large bowl, mix the rice flour, cornflour, caster sugar, turmeric and salt. Whisk in the egg and 250 ml (1 cup) of cold water and leave to sit for 5 minutes.

Fill a wok or medium-sized saucepan to about one-third full with oil and bring to 180°C or until a cube of bread dropped in the oil browns in 15 seconds.

Remove the bananas from the freezer and, working with one banana at a time, dip it in the batter, then carefully place in the oil and fry for 2 minutes on each side until just golden. Now the trick is to carefully remove the banana from the oil, allow it to drain on paper towel for a few minutes, then dip in the batter a second time and fry again for another 2–3 minutes on each side until golden brown (double-frying makes them wonderfully crunchy).

Drain the banana fritters on paper towel, then dust with icing sugar, drizzle with coconut cream and sprinkle over some peanuts. Eat warm or, if you're impatient like I am, eat them hot like the searing lava of Mt Vesuvius and try in vain to not burn the roof of your mouth.

'KEEP IT CLEANER' CHOC CHIP COOKIES

My friends Laura Henshaw and Steph Claire Smith (now Miller) have a wonderful community called Keep It Cleaner (or KIC). They have amazing recipes and great workouts to help young women. These incredible humans have always been so supportive of me and for that I love them. They really are the most caring individuals, always ready to help. I actually sent Steph a text three days before her wedding asking if she and Laura would be happy to share a recipe with me for this book (rude). Later that day, this came through, with images of the food and themselves for me. To my beautiful friends, thank you for being so generous, for always having my back and for this delicious recipe.

MAKES 12

85 g (⅓ cup) Greek yoghurt
2 tablespoons almond butter
6 medjool dates, roughly chopped
2 tablespoons rice malt syrup
1 teaspoon vanilla extract
3 tablespoons coconut oil
60 g almond meal
120 g gluten-free plain flour
1 teaspoon gluten-free baking
   powder
50 g dark chocolate (70% cocoa),
   finely chopped

Preheat the oven to 180°C. Line a large baking tray with baking paper.

Place the yoghurt, almond butter, dates, rice malt syrup, vanilla and coconut oil in a food processor and blitz to a paste.

Transfer to a large mixing bowl, then add the remaining ingredients and combine well.

Using a tablespoon, scoop the dough and roll into golf ball–sized balls. Place on the prepared tray and use the back of the spoon to gently press and flatten the dough.

Bake for 11–13 minutes until golden, then transfer to a wire rack to cool completely. These cookies will keep for up to 2 weeks in an airtight container.

CHERRY and COCONUT SLICE

Cherry and coconut are the Jay-Z and Beyoncé of the sweets world. It's one of my favourite pairings and one that has me drooling just at the thought of it. The use of condensed milk is a little nod to my heritage (us Vietnamese use it like it's going out of fashion). This slice is gluten free and, therefore, a foolproof dessert to bring to any gathering. Also, it's easily whipped up an hour before any event and it's a recipe my friends still beg me for. Well, here you go, guys! Plus the chocolate topping reminds me of the chocolate bars I used to swap my chippies for in primary school. Cute ... right?

SERVES 10–12

300 g glace cherries, chopped, plus extra to serve
375 g desiccated coconut, plus extra to serve
395 g can sweetened condensed milk
pinch of sea salt
200 g dark chocolate (70% cocoa), roughly chopped
2 tablespoons coconut oil

Line a 20 cm square slice tray with baking paper.

In a large mixing bowl, combine the cherries, coconut, condensed milk and salt. Press evenly into the prepared tray and pop in the freezer for 30 minutes to set.

Melt the chocolate and coconut oil in a heatproof bowl in the microwave for 30-second bursts, stirring between each burst. It should take 3–6 bursts, depending on the size of the chocolate pieces and the power of your microwave.

Pour the chocolate over the top of the cherry mixture, sprinkle with the extra cherries and coconut and pop in the fridge to set for at least 30 minutes.

Using a sharp knife, cut into pieces and serve. The slice will keep in an airtight container in the fridge for up to 1 week.

POP!

WHAT IS YOUR MUST—HAVE EQUIPMENT IN THE KITCHEN?

UMMM ... i'M ASSUMiNG WE ARE TALKiNG THiNGS THAT AREN'T ALWAYS COMMON, SO:

- A mandoline. These are dope once you get over the 'will I slice my finger off?' stage.
- A microplane, cause holy shit these are so convenient, but also they look kinda like 'Hey, I know what I'm doing' when you have people over and you are zesting a lemon or grating nutmeg.
- There are heaps more but actually a flame gun. Really good for finishing dishes. Adds a whole other level to your cooking. Torch some meringue or cured fish, or brulee anything. Like anything. I'm talking bananas, figs, custard, pancakes. Also looks sexy AF.

KLADDKAKA

My Swedish friend Oskar introduced me to the incredible world of kladdkaka one summer when he was holidaying in Melbourne. My friendship with Oskar is unique because, well, we only knew each other in person for about six weeks, but because of Instagram we still speak almost weekly. You know, the friendships where you write on each other's photos with supportive messages and positive affirmations.

Anyway, Oskar told me about this Swedish chocolate cake that his grandma would make, which was humble but decadent and really reminded him of home. Later that week I had him and a few friends over and I presented him with kladdkaka for dessert. I know how homesick travelling can make you and a little taste of home goes a long way. (He then spent 10 minutes trying to teach me how to pronounce it. Plot twist: I still get it wrong.)

I wanted to share this recipe because I serve it regularly (it's so yum!) and it always reminds me that while some friendships can be brief, that doesn't make them any less valuable.

P.S. Oskar, you're in my book, so now you have to let me crash on your couch when I visit.

SERVES 6

2 large eggs
280 g caster sugar
65 g plain flour
30 g (¼ cup) unsweetened cocoa powder, plus extra for dusting
pinch of sea salt
120 g butter, melted, plus extra for greasing
1 tablespoon vanilla bean paste
icing sugar, for dusting (optional)
thick cream, to serve
blackberries, to serve

Preheat the oven to 180°C. Grease a 20 cm springform cake tin with butter and dust the inside with cocoa powder.

In the bowl of a stand mixer fitted with a paddle attachment, beat the eggs and caster sugar until thick and pale in colour (this will make the cake gooey and fudge-like).

Sift the flour, cocoa and salt together into a bowl.

Gently fold the dry ingredients into the eggs and sugar. Mix in the melted butter and vanilla paste. Pour the batter into the cake tin and bake for 20–25 minutes until the top has hardened but the centre is still soft. You can test this by inserting a wooden skewer into the centre and seeing if comes out with little pieces of wet, sand-like crumbs. If it's fully coated then the cake isn't ready; if it comes out totally clean then you've taken it too far.

Remove the cake from the oven, release the springform and run a knife around the kladdkaka to help release it. Allow to cool slightly, dust with icing sugar (if you like) and leave to cool completely.

When you are ready to serve, lift the cake from the base of the springform onto a serving platter. Slice and serve with a generous dollop of cream and some blackberries.

THE FAMILY WE CHOOSE: COOKING FOR (AND WITH!) YOUR FRIENDS

TIP: THIS CAKE IS ALSO DELICIOUS SERVED WITH SOME STRAWBERRIES AND GOOD VANILLA ICE CREAM — OR VANILLA YOGHURT FOR A SLIGHTLY HEALTHIER OPTION. PERSONALLY, I LOVE KLADDKAKA WITH RASPBERRIES TOSSED WITH A SQUEEZE OF LIME, BECAUSE THEIR TARTNESS CUTS THROUGH THE RICH CHOCOLATE.

CHAPTER THREE

A BROKEN HEART

FOOD TO PICK YOU UP AFTER YOU'VE FALLEN

OMG, how annoying are break-ups? Okay, I get it, we aren't gonna get married, but can we just move on now? Well, apparently not. Four partners (three disastrous), too many dates to keep count of and even more deep and meaningful one-night relationships, the constant for me through all of this has been food. Food is the love of my life. It may sound funny to say I deal with break-ups through food, but I think that may be because I deal with everything through food.

For example, one of my exes (let's call him Brad) was coeliac. We ended on bad terms – I was broken, I was a mess, I stalked him like crazy on Instagram but I remember thinking 'OMG, at least I can eat gluten again without feeling bad', which was heaven because all I wanted was carbs. I wanted to cry, I wanted to watch movies all day and I wanted to indulge.

Another ex, one of my most recent partners, Thor ... yeah Thor, that's fitting. He cheated on me, he made me question everything about myself – my looks, my personality, my career choices and me in general. Was I not enough? (I am.) Was I too much? (No, sorry, busy.) Am I a psychopath? (Well, yes ...) Anyway, the break-up with Thor made me feel completely the opposite to my break-up with Brad. This break-up motivated me, it made me want to be fitter, stronger (physically and emotionally) and closer to my friends. I hosted more dinner parties, I went to brunches, I wanted to make things for other people. I also wanted to smash things, but there is a recipe in here for that too (check out my bang bang chicken on page 118).

This chapter is all about how food makes you feel; it's about reconnecting with your cravings and your emotions. Every break-up is different, so what we crave is always different and that's okay. Eat what you love – get happy again and cook food that makes you feel good. For me, it ranges from simple cacio e pepe (page 105) and salted caramel popcorn (for rom-com marathons, page 128) to my mum's chicken congee (page 123) and beautiful steak with a green chimichurri (page 126). The idea is that eating your feelings doesn't have to be about eating heaps of sugar, carbs or butter. It's about your cravings and finding food to satisfy those without feeling guilty afterwards, breaking the bank or spending six hours cooking ... because ain't nobody got time for that.

WHAT'S IN THIS CHAPTER?

♡ THIS CHAPTER IS FULL OF RECIPES THAT ARE FAST YET FULL OF FLAVOUR, DISHES THAT USE INGREDIENTS YOU WILL PROBABLY ALREADY HAVE IN YOUR PANTRY AND FRIDGE.

♡ THINK COMFORT FOODS, LIKE CRISPY POTATOES WITH ALL THE TRIMMINGS (PAGE 115) AND CHICKEN SOUP (PAGE 106).

♡ THERE'S STRAWBERRY BREAD (PAGE 138) THAT IS SO GOOD IT WILL MAKE AN ONION WANNA CRY, AND A CHOC-PEANUT TART (PAGE 139) THAT WILL SURELY FIX YOUR HEARTBREAK.

♡ THIS FOOD IS AS COMFORTING AS THE BLANKET YOU USED TO CARRY AROUND AS A TODDLER (I STILL HAVE MINE).

CACIO E PEPE

I cannot tell you how many bowls of cacio e pepe got me through my break-up with Brad. It was like I was making up for all the lost gluten I didn't consume during our relationship or something. Anyway, there was clearly something about the carbs, the creaminess of the cheese once mixed with the pasta water and the spice from the black pepper that was uber comforting. This recipe, even though it's just a handful of ingredients, is a flavour BOMBBBBB and I'm so glad it became my 'f*ck ya, I'm just gonna eat pasta and be happy' dish.

SERVES 2

200 g good-quality dried spaghetti
2 teaspoons freshly ground black pepper, plus extra to serve
150 g Pecorino Romano, finely grated
80 g parmesan, finely grated

TIP: THIS RECIPE SAYS IT'S FOR TWO BUT I'M PRETTY SURE I'D SMASH THIS AMOUNT ALL BY MYSELF, IT'S THAT GOOD.

Bring a saucepan of almost-too-salty water to the boil and cook the spaghetti according to the packet instructions (I like to cook it for 2 minutes less than what it says to so it's al dente). Drain the pasta but reserve the cooking water, as you'll need it for the sauce.

In a deep frying pan, toast the pepper over medium heat for 20–30 seconds until the spice tickles your nose. Ladle about 125 ml (½ cup) of the pasta water into the pan and add the pasta. Add the two cheeses and mix everything well (use tongs to stir the pasta or try to toss it together using the pan). Add another 125–250 ml (½–1 cup) of pasta water and mix until it all comes together into a thick, creamy, saucy-looking consistency.

Top with more pepper and serve the pasta into bowls if you want, but it's actually best eaten hot from the pan because the more it cools the more the cheese sets – unless you're into that, cause sometimes that's good, too.

CHINESE CHICKEN and CORN EGG-DROP SOUP

Let's talk about comfort. You know the chicken and sweet corn soup you get from your local Chinese takeaway shop? Yeah, so this is that dish. No matter how many Number 23s (black pepper beef), Number 31s (lemon chicken) or Number 44s (special fried rice) I order, I can never go past my loving, sweet, nutty and silky chicken and sweet corn soup. I love the familiar flavours of takeaway when I just CBF. This is a wholesome staple when I'm feeling down, and definitely a 'warm your belly and heart' kind of dish.

SERVES 4

1 skinless chicken breast
750 ml (3 cups) chicken stock, plus 3 tablespoons extra
1 teaspoon light soy sauce
½ teaspoon ground turmeric
1 teaspoon minced ginger
1 garlic clove, crushed
½ teaspoon sesame oil
1 tablespoon shaoxing (Chinese cooking wine)
225 g (1½ cups) thawed frozen sweet corn kernels, ½ cup roughly chopped
1½ tablespoons cornflour
1 egg, plus 1 egg white, lightly beaten
pinch of ground white pepper

TO SERVE
chopped coriander leaves
sliced spring onion
freshly ground black pepper

Place the chicken breast in a medium saucepan. Cover with cold water, then bring to the boil over high heat. Reduce the heat to low and simmer for 13–16 minutes until the juices run clear when the chicken is pierced with a knife. Set aside to cool, then shred into fine pieces.

Combine the chicken stock, soy sauce, turmeric, ginger, garlic, sesame oil, shaoxing and corn in a saucepan over high heat and bring to the boil.

Place the cornflour in a small bowl and, using chopsticks, mix with the extra chicken stock to make a slurry (lol). Give the corn mixture a stir and pour in the slurry (this thickens the soup).

Now, turn the heat off and, while gently stirring the soup in one direction, slowly pour in the beaten egg in a steady stream to form egg ribbons.

Stir in the shredded chicken, add the white pepper and serve in cute little bowls topped with a sprinkling of coriander, spring onion and black pepper.

TIP: ON THE DL, THIS WAS A GO-TO FOR ONE OF MY GIRLFRIENDS AND I AT THE END OF A BIG NIGHT OUT. STAY WITH ME HERE ... WE WOULD POP SOME VERY THIN BEAN-THREAD NOODLES INTO BOWLS, POUR THE SOUP OVER THE TOP AND MICROWAVE FOR 90 SECONDS SO THE NOODLES WOULD COOK. WE WOULD THEN LOAD IT WITH CORIANDER AND CRISPY SHALLOTS AND EAT WHILE WHISPERING SOU-OP TO EACH OTHER BEFORE WE PASSED OUT WITH FULL BELLIES.

TIPS: DROP THE LAP CHEONG FOR A VEGO VERSION.

IF YOU, UNLIKE ME, ACTUALLY LIKE THE TASTE OF UNCOOKED BEAN SPROUTS, ADD THEM TO YOUR BOWL INSTEAD OF THE WOK FOR ADDED CRUNCH. (THIS MAY BE A BIG CALL, BUT IN MY MIND RAW BEAN SPROUTS ARE WORSE THAN THE DEVIL.)

SMOKY SRIRACHA NOODS

Who doesn't love noods? Especially when your heart is broken. This recipe technically serves two, but it's really for one lonely heart (with leftovers for lunch), because when I'm down I need carbs, I need flavour, I need comfort and I need ease. For me, these smoky noods provide all this, and also they're done in less than 15 minutes and packed full of yum. The kecap manis is sweet and offsets the hot sriracha and salty soy so well. Hit it with freshness from the lime and this dish is an absolute banger.

SERVES 2

1 teaspoon vegetable oil
2 lap cheong (Chinese sausage), finely sliced
handful of garlic chives, chopped into 5 cm pieces (please, go to an Asian grocer and get these, or the internet will help you find them)
200 g cooked flat rice noodles (thick like your thumb)
2 teaspoons light soy sauce
1 teaspoon dark soy sauce
1 teaspoon kecap manis
1 teaspoon sriracha chilli sauce
2 eggs
45 g (½ cup) bean sprouts
1 tablespoon crushed Salted Peanuts (page 25)
2 teaspoons crispy fried shallots
2 lime wedges

Heat the oil in a wok over high heat. Add the lap cheong and cook for 1–2 minutes, tossing constantly. Add the garlic chives and noodles and give the pan a quick toss, then add the soy sauces, kecap manis and sriracha. Cook, tossing constantly, for 2 minutes, then leave to caramelise for 1 minute without touching it (if it looks like it's burning, that's good!).

Push the noodles to one side of the wok to make some room, then break the eggs into the space and cook, gently stirring, for 1 minute until the eggs are cooked. Toss well with the noodles, turn the heat off and toss the bean sprouts through.

Serve immediately into bowls and top with the crushed peanuts, fried shallots and lime wedges.

SEND NOODS!

GRILLED SUGARCANE PRAWNS

Over a summer break in my teens I had a horrific break up (because young love is hard, right?) and ran away with my fam to Vietnam for a few weeks. We stayed with Mum's side of the family and every afternoon this wonderful smoky–sweet smell would waft through my upstairs window where I was probably furiously rearranging my top friends on myspace or choosing a new page layout. This scent was from prawns made into a mousse, wrapped around little fingers of sugarcane and then grilled over coals. I ended up eating this most days as a snack before dinner, usually consuming so much that I would completely ruin my appetite (plot twist: I still ate dinner). This dish requires a bit more effort than many in this chapter, but to me it belongs here in comfort food, as it reminds me of that wonderful holiday, of eating to get through my break-up and of how food can make it all better.

SERVES 2-4

500 g raw prawns, peeled, deveined and chopped
3 spring onions, white parts only, finely sliced
2 teaspoons fish sauce
½ teaspoon garlic powder
1 teaspoon caster sugar
½ teaspoon sea salt
½ teaspoon freshly ground black pepper
1 sugarcane stick (see Tip)

TO SERVE

Spring Onion Oil (page 25)
Salted Peanuts (page 26)
crispy fried shallots
butter lettuce leaves (optional)
coriander, Vietnamese mint or mint leaves (optional)

Pulse the chopped prawn in a food processor until it forms a paste. Transfer to a mixing bowl, add the remaining ingredients except the sugarcane and mix well to combine.

Split the sugarcane into three equal parts, then peel and quarter each part – you should end up with 12 pieces of sugarcane.

Divide the prawn mixture into 12 equal portions, then press each portion around the middle of a piece of sugarcane.

Heat a barbecue grill (preferably charcoal) to high, or a chargrill pan over high heat.

Grill the sugarcane prawns for 2–3 minutes on each side or until nicely charred and cooked through.

Serve on a platter topped with the spring onion oil, salted peanuts and crispy shallots. When I feel like adding some freshness, I serve these with piles of lettuce leaves and herbs. I like to pull the prawn mixture off the sugarcane, place it on top of a lettuce leaf, top with herbs and lashings of spring onion oil, then finish with peanuts and shallots.

TIP: SUGARCANE CAN BE FOUND, FRESH OR FROZEN, AT YOUR LOCAL ASIAN GROCER. IF YOU BUY IT FROZEN IT'S USUALLY ALREADY CUT INTO SMALLER PIECES.

ASK ME A QUESTION

WHAT FOOD DON'T YOU UNDERSTAND?

THERE'S SO MUCH I DON'T UNDERSTAND. IT'S A CONSTANT LEARNING EXPERIENCE. LIKE THE OTHER DAY, I LEARNT HOW TO MAKE TADIG. HEAVEN. I ALSO DON'T UNDERSTAND:

- Why chicken soup is always better when my mum makes it.
- Why I can't stop myself from eating a whole punnet of blueberries.
- Why I get angry when people pick at food as I'm cooking it.
- Alfalfa. Like, ewwww ... why?
- Why packet noodles are bomb AF and I will never not love them.
- Why cornichons are so much better than gherkins. Like, aren't they just different sizes of the same thing?
- Who decided to be like, 'Oh look, bread, let's cook it again.' Like, how did toast happen? WTF.
- Why you don't write or text back. You chased me.

NAUGHTY CRISPY POTATOES

Potatoes: the over-achiever of vegetables – bringing us potato chips, fries, baked spuds, mash and even vodka. Who doesn't love a potato? So versatile and delicious in all its forms, at this point I feel like the other vegetables aren't even trying. This recipe is for the yummiest, hug-like baked potato, topped with all the trimmings – smoky bacon, salty parmesan, tangy sour cream and obviously chives because … greens. Make this recipe to accompany a roast, steak or even as a stand-alone dish.

Fun fact: once I forgot about them and left them in the oven for about half an hour more than I was supposed to and they turned out extra crispy. They were a little dry, but even a bad baked potato is good.

SERVES 4

1 kg baby red potatoes, skin on
2 garlic bulbs
3 tablespoons extra-virgin olive oil
sea salt
150 g bacon, diced
50 g (½ cup) grated parmesan
150 g sour cream
1 tablespoon chopped chives

Preheat the oven to 190°C.

Place the potatoes in a saucepan of heavily salted water (it's important to pop them into cold water, as it helps with not overcooking the outside of the potato). Bring to the boil over high heat and cook for 15–20 minutes or until they're easily pierced with a fork.

Drain the potatoes and place them in a heavy-based roasting tin. Crush them lightly using a potato masher. Slice the tops off the garlic bulbs and add them to the tin. Douse the potatoes and garlic with the oil and a good sprinkling of salt, then roast for 35–45 minutes until crispy. Check the potatoes after 30 minutes and then every 5 minutes to make sure they don't burn.

About 5 minutes before the potatoes are done, cook the bacon in a frying pan over medium–high heat for 3–5 minutes until crispy. Throw the bacon over the potatoes along with the parmesan and bake for another 5 minutes until the parmesan is melted and golden.

Dollop sour cream in all the gaps and crevices between the spuds, top with the chives, then eat it up and moan about being in a food coma.

BALINESE COCONUT and SNAKE BEAN SALAD

I fell in love with Bali back in 2007 when I first went with my family on a two-week holiday. What followed was basically a yearly love affair. As I got older, I returned for the food even more than the weather and beaches. Mama San and Sarong for the curries, Bambu for a touch of modern Indonesian food and Métis if you're fancy like that. Towards my mid-twenties, I got more adventurous and started eating street-side and out of the baskets sitting on street hawkers' heads. This is my Bali now. The little banana-leaf parcels of rice and meat? Yum!!! The last few times I've been to Bali, though, it was to attend health retreats. With my new busy schedule, I try to kill multiple birds with one stone: holiday/food/fitness. Sign me up. At one particular retreat, I developed an obsession with this salad. It's a Balinese staple and I loved it so much that I harassed the chef into showing me how he made it. I've changed a few things, but it's the wonderful coconut that really makes this dish. Eat it as a main or as part of a larger feast — either way, it is so tasty that it will lift absolutely any mood.

SERVES 2

250 g snake beans, cut 5 mm pieces
1 carrot, cut into matchsticks
100 g bean sprouts
1 tablespoon coconut oil
4 red shallots, sliced
2 garlic cloves, sliced
2 long red chillies, sliced
6 makrut lime leaves (see page 13), finely chopped
1 tablespoon fish sauce
1 cup (firmly packed) freshly grated coconut
pinch of sea salt
juice of ½ lime

Blanch the snake beans, carrot and bean sprouts for 1–2 minutes in boiling water, then drain well. Set aside.

Melt the coconut oil in a large frying pan over medium heat. Add the shallot, garlic, half the chilli and the lime leaf and cook for 3–4 minutes until fragrant. Add the fish sauce and stir well to deglaze the pan, then turn off the heat and stir in the grated coconut.

Toss the blanched veggies into the pan, then add the remaining chilli and the salt. Finish with a squeeze of lime and transfer to a serving dish.

A BROKEN HEART: FOOD TO PICK YOU UP AFTER YOU'VE FALLEN

BANG BANG SICHUAN CHICKEN

I have no idea why, but when people think of bang bang chicken they seem to think of a fried dish. But I know bang bang as chicken that is very gently poached and then pounded to get out all your frustrations. This dish was an instant favourite after my break-up with Thor a few years back. I was angry and I wanted to smash and scream and just be an absolute handful. Anyway, back to the food. The freshness and crunch from the cucumber perfectly balances out the hot, salty, numbing umami flavour of the Sichuan sauce. Don't worry, it's hot but not 'I can't taste anything' hot.

SERVES 2

5–7 cm piece of ginger, sliced
2 spring onions, whites trimmed, green parts finely sliced and reserved for the sauce
1 onion, quartered
2 small skinless chicken breasts or 1 large one (about 350 g in total)
½ cucumber, deseeded and finely sliced into batons

SICHUAN SAUCE
2 tablespoons light soy sauce
1 tablespoon Chinese black vinegar
2 tablespoons caster sugar
2 tablespoons sesame oil
1 tablespoon chilli oil
3 tablespoons toasted sesame seeds
1 teaspoon ground Sichuan peppercorns
½ teaspoon sea salt

Place the ginger, spring onion whites, onion and 500 ml (2 cups) of water in a saucepan and bring to the boil over high heat. Add the chicken breasts and bring back to the boil, then cover and turn to the lowest heat to poach gently for 11–14 minutes until the chicken is cooked. (To test, pierce the chicken with a skewer – the juices should run clear.) Plunge the chicken into an ice bath to stop it cooking and set the poaching liquid aside.

To make the Sichuan sauce, combine the ingredients in a bowl with the spring onion greens and 125 ml (½ cup) of the poaching liquid and set aside.

Shred the chicken (but not too finely) and pound (bang bang!) with a rolling pin to make flat thin pieces. Arrange the cucumber on two serving plates, then top with the chicken. Pour over the sauce and serve.

A BROKEN HEART: FOOD TO PICK YOU UP AFTER YOU'VE FALLEN

FEEL FREE TO SEASON THE PASTA WITH YOUR SALTY TEARS. LOL.

SPAGHETTI for ONE

Spaghetti bolognese is an essential for your cooking repertoire. It's often a dish people make when they first learn to cook and it's always great. Although, people usually cheat and use pre-made pasta sauce. DON'T! Instead, try this recipe. It's a faster bolognese than my slow and steady spag bol (page 78). I make this when I wanna look and feel like I have my shit together. An easy dinner that creates leftovers for lunch – a lunch I can bring into the office to have someone comment on how it's a different colour to my usual spag bol. (Shut up Karen, nobody asked you. Let me have my spaghetti in peace – it's the only thing standing between me and a complete mental breakdown.) Okay, back to the food. The tomato paste and oregano really boost this hearty dish and the fresh basil at the end really lifts it, too. My favourite thing about this recipe, though, is the bottle of red I insist you open to make the dish, which you really should polish off during the cooking process. Why is tipsy cooking not a TV show?

SERVES 1 (WITH LEFTOVERS FOR LUNCH THE NEXT DAY)

1 tablespoon extra-virgin olive oil
1 small onion, finely chopped
2 garlic cloves, crushed
250 g beef mince
2 tablespoons tomato paste
1 tablespoon dried oregano
400 ml passata
100 ml of your favourite red wine (one that you'll also be drinking, obvs)
handful of basil leaves, plus extra to serve (optional)
sea salt and freshly ground black pepper
150 g dried spaghetti
as much grated parmesan as you want

Start by popping the oil into a large deep saucepan over medium heat. Add the onion and cook, stirring, for 3 minutes or until softened and semi translucent. Add the garlic and cook for 30 seconds.

Throw the beef mince into the pan and cook, stirring, for 5–6 minutes until the beef is browned and no longer pink. Next goes the tomato paste and oregano – mix well, then add the passata and red wine (and pour yourself a glass to sip while you cook).

Reduce the heat to a simmer and leave uncovered to cook for 15 minutes (it's important to let the sauce and the other ingredients become good friends at this point). Add the basil and some salt and pepper and stir well.

Meanwhile, bring a large saucepan of heavily salted water to the boil. Cook the pasta according to the packet instructions (I like to cook mine for 1–1½ minutes less for that al dente bite). Drain and throw the pasta into the sauce. Make yourself a bowlful, top with parmesan and if you wanna Instagram it, a bit of extra basil. #nightsin

A BROKEN HEART: FOOD TO PICK YOU UP AFTER YOU'VE FALLEN

CHICKEN CONGEE with CRUNCHY CABBAGE SALAD

CHAO GOI GA

This is my version of chicken soup. It's a dish I make when I need to feel comforted, to feel loved and to make me feel better if I'm sick. It's wholesome, filling and always puts a huge smile on my face. Crunchy salad on the side of warm, sweet congee is like a big hug. I actually don't really make this for myself, because usually I call Mum to complain and ask her to make it for me.

SERVES 6

1 x 1.5 kg whole chicken
1 onion, peeled and halved
½ daikon, peeled and halved
4 cm piece of ginger, smashed
2 red shallots, peeled
sea salt
150 g (2 cups) shredded green cabbage
75 g (1 cup) shredded purple cabbage
1 carrot, shredded
1 red onion, finely sliced
1 cup Vietnamese mint leaves
½ cup coriander leaves
80 ml (⅓ cup) Nuoc Mam Dipping Sauce (page 34), plus extra to serve
3 tablespoons crispy fried shallots, plus extra to serve
2 tablespoons crushed Salted Peanuts (page 26), plus extra to serve
gio chao quay, to serve (optional; see Tip)

CONGEE
100 g (½ cup) jasmine rice, rinsed, soaked for 1 hour and drained
100 g (½ cup) glutinous rice, rinsed, soaked for 1 hour and drained
1 tablespoon caster sugar
1 tablespoon fish sauce
2 teaspoons chicken stock powder

Bring 10 litres of water to the boil in a large stockpot over high heat. Place the whole chicken in the water and blanch for 3 minutes to remove impurities. Drain.

Return the chicken to the stockpot along with the onion, daikon, ginger, shallots and a large pinch of salt and cover with 10 litres of cold water. Bring to the boil over high heat and skim off any foam that rises to the surface. Reduce the heat to medium–low, then simmer gently for 35–50 minutes, skimming off any foam, until the chicken is just cooked. Remove the chicken from the liquid using tongs (don't drain the stockpot, as you'll use the stock to cook the congee). To check that it's cooked, pierce the chicken above the thigh with a skewer – if the juice runs clear, it's ready. Transfer the chicken to an ice bath to stop the cooking process. Shred the meat and set aside for the salad.

Meanwhile, add all the congee ingredients to the cooking liquid in the stockpot. Boil for 10 minutes, then turn the heat off and leave, covered, for at least 30 minutes – don't touch it!

While your congee is sitting, make the salad. Combine the shredded chicken with the cabbage, carrot, red onion and herbs. Transfer to a large serving platter and dress with the nuoc mam. Top with the shallots and peanuts.

When you are ready to serve, turn the heat back to high under the congee, bring to the boil and cook for 5 minutes to heat through.

Transfer the congee into bowls and top with some extra fried shallots and salted peanuts, if you like. Serve with the cabbage salad, a bowl of extra nuoc mam and, if you like, some gio chao quay for dipping.

TIP: GIO CHAO QUAY IS VIETNAMESE FRIED BREAD, A BIT LIKE A SAVOURY DOUGHNUT. YOU CAN BUY IT FROM VIETNAMESE BAKERIES AND SOMETIMES FROM THE FREEZER SECTION OF ASIAN GROCERS.

CHICKEN CONGEE
WITH CRUNCHY CABBAGE
SALAD (PAGE 123)

JUST LIKE A BIG HUG :)

STEAK and CHIMI

When you're feeling down, sometimes all you need is a good steak and an even better sauce. I make this recipe a lot, for friends, family or even as a share-style dish that I pop in the middle of the table as a starter. It just makes you feel good, and I think food should always nourish your soul as much as your body. I have an ex who hated steak (honestly, what kind of meat-eater hates steak?), so I spent a good six months not really eating it. As soon as we broke up this was the first thing I made. I always choose steak on the bone because there is just so much more flavour. The zingy sauce is the perfect way to finish the steak; the green herbs and chillies look like they dance in the oil as you spoon it over the meat. Delish!

SERVES 2 (OR MORE AS PART OF A SHARED MEAL)

800 g T-bone or bone-in
    porterhouse (look for a steak
    that's about 3 cm thick)
sea salt
1 tablespoon unsalted butter
1 tablespoon extra-virgin olive oil
2 garlic cloves, unpeeled and lightly
    crushed with the back of a knife
3 thyme sprigs

CHIMICHURRI

1 red shallot, chopped
1 long red chilli, chopped
3 garlic cloves, roughly chopped
80 ml (⅓ cup) red wine vinegar
½ cup chopped coriander leaves
⅓ cup chopped flat-leaf parsley
    leaves
1 tablespoon chopped oregano
    leaves
generous pinch of sea salt
185 ml (¾ cup) extra-virgin olive oil

Remove your steak from the fridge and allow to sit at room temperature for 30–45 minutes (this helps with even cooking). Season the steak with a generous pinch of salt on each side.

Melt the butter with the oil in a heavy-based frying pan over high heat. Add the steak and cook for 2 minutes, then reduce the heat to medium and cook for a further 2 minutes on each side.

Add the garlic and thyme and use a spoon to baste the steak with the juices in the pan for 1 minute. Remove the steak from the pan and pop aside to rest, covered, for 5 minutes.

To make the chimi, pop all the ingredients except the oil in a food processor. Blitz until the mixture forms a rough paste. Add the oil and give it another quick blitz just to incorporate.

Slice up your steak and transfer to a serving board. Spoon over half the chimi and place the rest in a serving dish. A pinch of salt goes over the top and bang! You're in heaven.

SALTED CARAMEL POPCORN

Popcorn is truly one of my addictions. Even though I'm intolerant to corn, I love it. I've always popped the corn from scratch, because I find the flavour is better and I personally think everyone should know how to do it – it's ridiculously easy and so rewarding. I like to use a combination of oil and butter, because the oil stops the butter from burning and you get this nutty buttery popcorn as the final result. YUM!

SERVES 4 AS A SNACK FOR MOVIE NIGHT

3 tablespoons neutral oil (such as vegetable oil)
60 g salted butter
100 g good-quality popping corn kernels
sea salt
150 g caster sugar
1½ teaspoons bicarbonate of soda, sifted

Heat the oil and half the butter in a large saucepan over high heat for 2–3 minutes until the butter melts and starts to bubble. Pour in the corn kernels and cover with a lid. When you hear the first kernels pop, turn the heat down to medium and gently shake the pan and cook until all the kernels have popped (this usually takes 3–5 minutes).

Pour the popped corn into a large bowl and sprinkle with sea salt. You can stop here and start eating if you just want buttery, salty popcorn. If you're all in for the salted caramel, set the popcorn aside.

Line a baking tray with baking paper.

Clean out the saucepan and place over high heat. Add the sugar and 2 tablespoons of water. Leave for about 5–10 minutes so the sugar melts and caramelises to a deep amber colour – do not stir or the sugar will crystallise. The darker the colour, the more bitter the caramel flavour will be.

Once the caramel reaches the colour you desire, add the remaining butter and two large pinches of salt and mix well. Stir in the bicarb soda and watch as the caramel foams up, then add the popcorn back in and mix well.

Pour the caramel popcorn over the prepared tray and leave to cool and harden for at least 10 minutes. Break up the popcorn and serve.

SUNDAY CREPES

In 2019, I was going through a break-up while *RuPaul's Drag Race* was airing – a show I used to watch with my ex. Knowing this, my friend Olivier invited me over for a viewing party at his. It was a small group of about half-a-dozen gay men. It became a regular occurrence and during these viewing parties, Olivier would make crepes and lay out an assortment of toppings and fillings, from sweet to savoury. Olivier explained that in France, where he was from, every Sunday his family would make crepes for lunch – I just thought it was brilliant and so cute. It meant instead of spending hours cooking, you spent hours talking and laughing over a DIY lunch.

SERVES 4–6
(MAKES 12–16 CREPES)

310 ml (1¼ cups) milk, plus extra if necessary
4 large eggs
3 tablespoons melted butter, plus extra for cooking
150 g (1 cup) plain flour, sifted
2 teaspoons caster sugar
pinch of sea salt

CHOOSE-YOUR-OWN-
ADVENTURE TOPPINGS
shaved ham
grated cheese (I love comte and gruyere)
cornichons
smashed avo (see page 191 for my recipe)
dijon mustard
Vegemite
halved cherry tomatoes
Nutella
peanut butter
sliced strawberries
icing or caster sugar
lemon wedges
crushed toasted walnuts

Place the milk, eggs, butter, flour, sugar and salt in a blender to blend (duh). Whiz it up and check the consistency, adding a little more milk if you need. The batter shouldn't be too thick, but it also shouldn't be watery, like the consistency of a protein shake. Leave the batter to rest for 20 minutes.

Heat a large frying pan over medium heat and add a tiny bit of butter. Ladle in 3 tablespoons of batter, swirling the pan to spread out the batter, then cook for 30 seconds on each side before tipping onto a plate. Like pancakes, the first crepe is always a bit of a fail so you can sacrifice that one as a taster for seasoning – gently stir some more salt into the batter if needed. Repeat the cooking steps with the remaining batter, piling your crepes up on the plate (they'll look uber cute). Keep the crepes covered with a clean tea towel while you're cooking so they don't dry out.

To serve, create a spread at your table with whichever topping ingredients take your fancy, placed in cute serving bowls (or leave them in jars). Let everyone choose their own adventure, but my go-to to start would be a crepe with Vegemite, cheese and cherry tomatoes and to finish, a classic lemon juice and sugar crepe … GIVE ME!

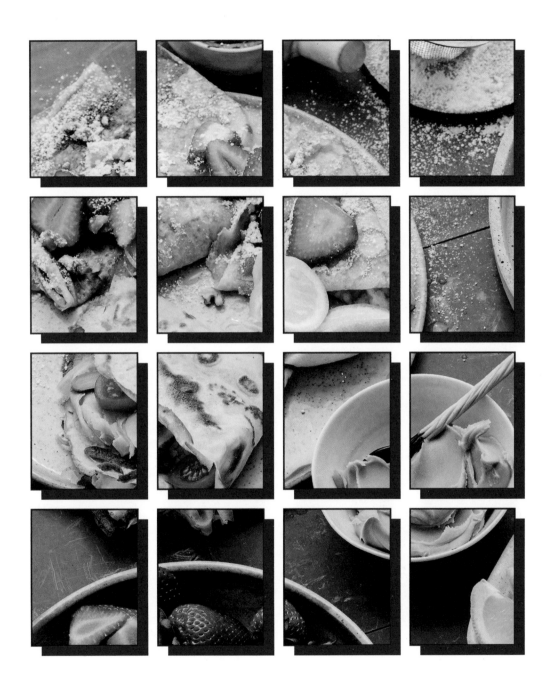

SUNDAY CREPES (PAGE 130)

MMMM...
GIVE ME!

TIPS FOR COOKING FOR ONE?

(I'M JUST OUT OF A FOUR-YEAR RELATIONSHIP.)

- Make sure you have staples in your pantry like canned beans, pasta and grains. Your fridge should have eggs, fats and, for me, protein. Then at the market, get seasonal veg and herbs, ready for your week. But remember to look at your week. If you're out three days, what's the point of buying 3 kg of greens?

- Remember to love your freezer, too. Obviously sometimes you can't cook for one, but what you can do is freeze things you've made for an easy meal later in the week. Just don't forget the meals or ingredients and leave them in your freezer.

- Another thing. You know how you're always like, 'I need to eat healthy'? Well, you typically tend to eat what is on hand. So stock your fridge and pantry with healthy foods and cook knowing you'll snack on these items.

- Lastly, leftover veg is my favourite end-of-the-week meal. It's like, chop that shit up, throw it on a baking tray and pop it in the oven with garlic, onion and hearty herbs for yum roast veg. Or brown off some onions and saute any root veg and celery (there's always celery) in a pot with oil. Add stock to deglaze and throw in your remaining leftover veg. Cook till tender, blitz it up and you have a yummo soup for lunch for the next four days.

SWEET AND TANGY STRAWBERRY BREAD (PAGE 138)

SWEET and TANGY STRAWBERRY BREAD

Move over banana bread, there's a new player in town! It's moist, sassy and totally down for a lazy Sunday on the couch. Exactly what you need when dealing with the fallout of a shitty relationship. This loaf is fluffy, light and absolutely mouth-watering, and you can put it on ice (in the freezer) if you feel like it's getting too clingy. Slice it up in individual pieces and pop it into the freezer for rainy or ugly-cry days. The tang from the buttermilk, yoghurt and strawberries offsets the sweetness in the loaf, so pop some butter on this and call it a night.

P.S. I may or may not have eaten half a loaf of this in one afternoon, one slice at a time.

SERVES 10

115 g (½ cup) caster sugar
60 g (⅓ cup lightly packed) brown sugar
1 egg
125 g (½ cup) Greek yoghurt
125 ml (½ cup) buttermilk
80 ml (⅓ cup) melted coconut oil
1½ teaspoons vanilla bean paste
300 g (2 cups) plain flour
1 teaspoon bicarbonate of soda
½ teaspoon sea salt
300 g strawberries, hulled, 50 g halved and the rest roughly chopped
icing sugar, for dusting

Preheat the oven to 180°C. Grease and line a 20 cm loaf tin.

Combine the sugars and egg in the bowl of a stand mixer fitted with the paddle attachment and beat for 3–5 minutes until pale and creamy. Add the yoghurt, buttermilk, coconut oil and vanilla paste. Beat for another minute until well combined.

Sift the flour, bicarb and salt into a large mixing bowl. Slowly pour the wet ingredients into the dry ingredients and mix well until there are no lumps.

Fold the chopped strawberries into the batter, then pour into the prepared tin. Top with the halved strawberries.

Bake for 45 minutes, then cover with foil and bake for another 15 minutes until a skewer inserted into the middle comes out clean. Allow to cool briefly in the tin then invert onto a wire rack to cool completely.

Dust with icing sugar, slice and enjoy. Store in an airtight container in the fridge for up to 1 week, or slice and store in the freezer for up to 3 months.

PICTURED ON PAGES 136–7

WICKEDLY GOOD 'SNICKERS' TART

Peanut butter, chocolate and condensed milk! This is an absolute treat, an incredibly rich tart that will mend even the most broken of hearts ... well, it doesn't really, but it's yum AF. Make this, cut it up into slices, gram it, then eat half the thing while watching old eps of *Friends* (I may be talking from personal experience).

SERVES 8

275 g cream-filled chocolate cookies (such as Oreos)
80 ml (⅓ cup) melted butter
½ teaspoon sea salt
3 tablespoons roughly chopped Salted Peanuts (page 26)

PEANUT BUTTER CARAMEL
125 g butter
95 g (½ cup lightly packed) brown sugar
395 g can sweetened condensed milk
125 ml (½ cup) pure cream
1 teaspoon sea salt
250 g (1 cup) smooth peanut butter

CHOCOLATE TOPPING
150 g milk chocolate
75 ml pure cream

Preheat the oven to 160°C. Line the base of a 23 cm tart tin with baking paper.

Place the cookies, butter and salt in a food processor and blitz to a wet, sand-like consistency. Press the crumb into the base and side of the tart tin and set aside.

To make the peanut butter caramel, melt the butter in a saucepan over medium–high heat. Stir in the brown sugar and cook for 6–8 minutes until it starts to bubble. Add the condensed milk and cream, then turn off the heat and stir in the salt and peanut butter. (Usually at this point I'll eat half the caramel. Don't be me, save it for the tart.)

Now pour the peanut butter caramel into the tart base and pop into the oven for 15 minutes. You're looking for it to bubble and thicken. Remove the tart from the oven and leave to cool for 30 minutes.

To make the chocolate topping, all you need to do is melt the chocolate and cream – I usually just pop them in a bowl and microwave for 30-second blasts, giving it a stir in between each blast, until melted and combined (it usually takes 1½–2 minutes in total).

Pour the chocolate topping over the tart, then sprinkle with the peanuts and some extra salt, if you like. Pop in the fridge for about 1 hour to set. Slice and devour. Store any leftovers in an airtight container in the pantry for 5 days, or in the fridge for up to 10 days.

PICTURED ON PAGES 140–1

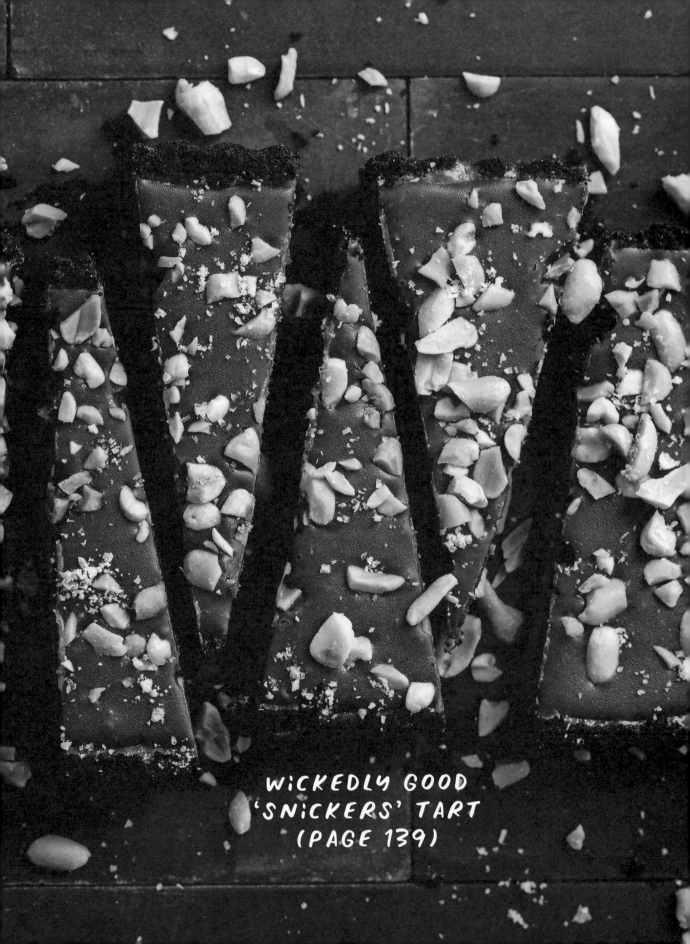

WICKEDLY GOOD
'SNICKERS' TART
(PAGE 139)

CHAPTER FOUR

SUSTAINABLE DATING

EASY MEALS THAT LOOK IMPRESSIVE AF
AND TASTE YUM

It's 2020 and for some reason people are scared to go on a date. I'm not talking 'catch-ups, drinks or Netflix and chill'. I'm talking, 'Hey, I'm into you and I would like to take you out, make you dinner or go kayaking' (don't knock it till you try it).

The last couple of years for me has been about making my intentions clear. I go into every date thinking, 'Could this man be my future partner?' I know it sounds intense but we are all thinking it; if you're not then why waste your time?

Dating for me has always been very old school. I'm a hopeless romantic who believes in happily-ever-after and soulmates (even though I feel like soulmates and lovers are very different things). Nothing makes me happier than cooking or being cooked for on a date, it gives you time to talk and have a wine while making a delicious meal. It's also great because you don't need to worry about starting convos – I feel like there's always something to talk about over food.

Sustainable dating is just that – easy dishes that look impressive AF, are yum and leave time for you to get to know the person you're with. Some of these recipes actually come from things I've cooked for a partner or love interest. This chapter is sexy, moody and just the right amount of fancy. It ranges from first-date dishes to couch-date bowls, morning-after-date brunches and sweets for your sweetie.

The chapters in this book are like little babies for me and I know you're not supposed to have favourites, but I have a love for this chapter that is different from the others. For me, this is a rollercoaster of emotions, with dishes that remind me of the great times and also dishes that remind me of the exes I made them for. If you're cooking for a potential someone special or a long-term partner, this is the chapter for you.

WHAT'S IN THIS CHAPTER?

♡ MEALS THAT ARE PERFECT FOR COUCH DATES, LIKE MY THAI GREEN CURRY (PAGE 160) OR SHAKING BEEF (HANDS-DOWN FAVE EVER, PAGE 174).

♡ DISHES TO PICK AT WHILE YOU CHIT CHAT, LIKE MY DIPS (PAGES 146–7) OR GRILLED OCCY WITH CRISPY CAPERS (PAGE 169).

♡ WANT SOMETHING UBER IMPRESSIVE? TRY MY VEGEMITE AND CHICKEN DUMPLINGS (PAGE 168) OR DRUNK AND STICKY DATE PUD (PAGE 182).

♡ YOU'LL ALSO FIND DISHES THAT ARE A LITTLE BIT LEFT OF CENTRE HERE TOO, LIKE MY GREEN CURRY PRAWN TOAST (PAGE 162) AND CHOCOLATE HONEYCOMB (PAGE 179).

DIP, DIP or DIP?

One of my favourite things to do for a first date is to have a board full of grazing things, such as dips, crudités, good bread, crackers, nuts and other nibbles. I think this is the perfect way of eating when you just want to have a chilled drink, slowly picking at the platter or board. These three dips are all plant based, great for making ahead of time and keeping in an airtight container ready to be used. Just make sure you bring them to room temp before serving,

P.S. These dips all go really well in a sandwich, too.

SERVES 2 AS AN IMPRESSIVE SPREAD

HUMMUS

3 tablespoons lemon juice
90 g (⅓ cup) tahini
1 large garlic clove, crushed
2 tablespoons extra-virgin olive oil, plus extra to serve
½ teaspoon ground cumin
400 g can chickpeas, rinsed and drained
2–4 tablespoons iced water
sea salt
sumac, to serve
chopped flat-leaf parsley leaves, to serve

In a food processor, blitz the lemon juice and tahini for 30 seconds. Add the garlic, olive oil and cumin and blitz again until combined.

Add half the chickpeas and blitz for 30 seconds. Scrape down the side, then add the rest of the chickpeas and blitz until combined.

At this point the dip will be coarse and dry, so, with the motor running, add the iced water 1 tablespoon at a time until the mixture gets to the texture you want. Add all 4 tablespoons if you like your hummus really smooth and creamy.

Season with salt and transfer the hummus to a serving bowl. Drizzle some olive oil over the top and sprinkle with sumac, salt and chopped parsley.

ROASTED CAPSICUM DIP

155 g (1 cup) cashews, soaked in water overnight then drained
3 red capsicums
5 garlic cloves, unpeeled
1 tablespoon extra-virgin olive oil, plus extra to serve
½ teaspoon smoked paprika, plus extra to serve
sea salt

Pop the cashews in a food processor.

Place the capsicums and garlic cloves on a wire rack and place over the gas hob on your stovetop (or on a gas barbecue if you don't have a gas stove). Turn the gas to high and char the capsicums and garlic, turning often, until the skins blacken all over (this should take about 15 minutes).

Place the capsicums in a bowl, cover with plastic wrap and set aside to steam for 10–15 minutes. Remove the skins from the garlic and pop the cloves in the food processor with the cashews.

Remove the skins, stems and seeds from the capsicums (the skins should just rub off) and place the flesh in the food processor. Add the olive oil, smoked paprika and a pinch of salt and blitz for 30 seconds on high. Add a little water, 1 tablespoon at a time, until you get the consistency you like.

Transfer the dip to a serving bowl and finish with a little extra olive oil and smoked paprika.

MUSHROOM PATE

1 tablespoon extra-virgin olive oil
1 onion, finely chopped
4 garlic cloves, crushed
300 g Swiss brown or button mushrooms, sliced
3 tablespoons chopped flat-leaf parsley leaves
2 teaspoons chopped rosemary leaves
1 teaspoon thyme leaves
100 g (1 cup) toasted walnuts
2 tablespoons nutritional yeast
1 teaspoon sea salt
½ teaspoon freshly ground black pepper

Heat the olive oil in a large heavy-based frying pan over medium heat. Add the onion and cook for 5 minutes or until softened. Add the garlic and cook for a further minute. Add the mushroom, parsley, rosemary and thyme and saute, stirring, for 6–9 minutes until the mushroom has lightly browned and reduced in size.

Transfer to a food processor and add the walnuts, nutritional yeast, salt and pepper. Blitz to a paste.

Transfer to a serving dish, cover with plastic wrap and leave in the fridge to cool completely before serving.

ROASTED CAPSICUM DIP

MUSHROOM PATE

HUMMUS

2-MINUTE MAYO

Why, oh why, do I have a whole spread dedicated to mayo? Well, two reasons: first, mayo is SO easy and quick to make; and second, it is so frickin' impressive when done in front of a guest. What I usually do is invite a new love interest over for dinner, we chat, have some wine while I'm cooking (apron on, tea towel on my shoulder ... yes, this is my move). Then, just before I'm ready to serve, I 'realise' I've forgotten the mayo to go with our dinner. I whip out the stick blender, make this simple mayo and my date is now obsessed with the fact that I'm a wizard. Works every time. Usually there's a small convo about how cool mayo is, we eat, we laugh and no one needs to know I've planned it (except all of you who've now read this).

MAKES AROUND 400 G

1 egg
2 teaspoons dijon mustard
2 teaspoons white wine vinegar
juice of ½ lemon
large pinch of sea salt
300 ml neutral oil (such
    as grapeseed)

Crack the egg carefully into the blending container that comes with your stick blender (if you don't have the container, you just want something with high sides and a small base – like a measuring jug). Add the mustard, vinegar, lemon juice and salt. Lower the stick blender into the container, but not all the way to the bottom, so the egg remains unbroken. Add the oil and blitz, lifting the blender up out of the container as you do so. Once you can see ribbons of creamy mayo forming, put the blender down the bottom of the container to incorporate the egg.

Continue to blitz for 30 seconds until everything has smoothly emulsified into a thick mayo, lifting the blender as you go to ensure everything's well combined. The mayo will keep in an airtight container in the fridge for 3–5 days.

TIP: SO, THIS IS THE BASE RECIPE FOR PLAIN MAYO, WHICH YOU CAN MAKE SEXY AF BY ADDING LIME ZEST TO MAKE A LIME MAYO OR SMOKED PAPRIKA, CUMIN AND CORIANDER OR EVEN ANCHOVIES. SIMPLY ADD YOUR FLAVOURINGS BEFORE ADDING THE OIL. THIS RECIPE IS VERSATILE SO HAVE FUN WITH IT. IF YOU CHOOSE TO USE INGREDIENTS THAT MIGHT RELEASE LIQUID, SUCH AS FRESH HERBS, YOU MAY NEED TO ADD MORE OIL TO HELP IT EMULSIFY. ONCE YOU GET THE HANG OF MAKING THIS MAYO, YOU CAN ALSO ADD FLAVOURED OIL. FOR EXAMPLE, I MAKE A CHILLI OIL (SEE PAGE 13) AND THEN USE THAT TO MAKE THE MAYO, TO GET THAT CHILLI FLAVOUR INTO A CREAMIER SAUCE.

WALNUT and BLUE CHEESE SALAD

If I had a chapter called 'annoy your partner', this recipe would be in it. I made this for date night after fighting with a man about blue cheese. He said it sucked, I said it was incredible, so after a few back and forths I snuck it into a salad. The secret here is the deep nuttiness of the walnuts, the bitterness from the witlof and the sweetness from the vanilla that perfectly balances out the funk of the cheese. He ended up loving it and, therefore, I win. Sustainable dating is obviously all about compromise (or in this case tricking my other half into seeing things my way … classic Scorpio).

SERVES 2

80 g (⅓ cup) vanilla yoghurt
2 witlof, trimmed and leaves
  separated
1 packham pear, halved, cored and
  finely sliced
120 g toasted walnuts
100 g of your favourite blue cheese
  (not too gooey)
2½ tablespoons extra-virgin
  olive oil
1½ tablespoons balsamic vinegar
pinch of sea salt

Spread the yoghurt over a serving platter, then arrange the witlof over it, followed by the pear. Top with the walnuts and roughly tear bits of blue cheese over (I do this so I can eat the cheese that gets stuck to my fingers after).

Drizzle with the olive oil and then the balsamic (I don't mix them first because I like seeing the balsamic drip off the leaves). Finish with a generous sprinkling of salt.

LOVERS' SALAD ♂→

♡

My lovers' salad was born because I fell in love with bitter leaves a few years ago. I feel like when you're young you detest the taste of anything with bitterness in it, but as you get older, bitter is yum! Layers of beautiful purples, pinks and reds make this dish so sexy, and a nice hit of sweet and sour from the dressing with creaminess from the ricotta perfectly balance out the bitter leaves. It's a lovers' salad because I made it for a man-baby who 'couldn't even' with radicchio, so I had to balance the bitter leaves to trick him into loving it, like a child.

SERVES 2

½ radicchio, leaves separated
1 small red witlof, leaves separated
1 tablespoon extra-virgin olive oil
150 g strawberries, trimmed and sliced
sea salt and freshly ground black pepper
200 g good-quality fresh ricotta
2½ tablespoons toasted pine nuts
seeds from 1 small pomegranate

BLOOD ORANGE DRESSING

3 blood oranges
1 tablespoon lemon juice
2½ tablespoons maple syrup
½ teaspoon orange blossom water
sea salt and freshly ground black pepper

To make the dressing, segment two of the oranges (do this over a bowl to catch any juice) and set the segments aside. Squeeze the leftover membrane from the segmented oranges into a small saucepan, along with the juice from the remaining orange and any juice you caught while cutting. Add the rest of the ingredients to the pan and simmer over medium heat for 15–20 minutes until the dressing has reduced to a thick syrup (you should be left with about 3 tablespoons).

Tear the radicchio leaves into large pieces and place in a mixing bowl. Add the witlof leaves, olive oil, strawberry and some salt and pepper. Toss well, then transfer to a serving platter.

Arrange the reserved blood orange segments on the platter, dollop on the ricotta and finish with the dressing, pine nuts and pomegranate seeds.

SRIRACHA and COCONUT CAULIFLOWER

'Why do you never cook vegan food?' This was the question that gave birth to this sassy rebuttal cauliflower dish. After being hassled a few times on my social media I decided I would throw a dinner party that was completely vegan (I'm petty like that). This was also the inspo behind my plant-based dips on pages 146–7. This spicy cauliflower makes a great stand-alone meal or side dish. It's sexy, colourful and perfect for those date nights when you want a light dinner so you can fill up on wine and each other's company instead.

SERVES 2-4

2 tablespoons melted coconut oil
3 teaspoons light soy sauce
3 teaspoons rice wine vinegar
2 tablespoons sriracha chilli sauce,
    plus extra to serve
3 tablespoons canned coconut milk
2 teaspoons smoked paprika
1 head of cauliflower (about 800 g),
    sliced into 1.5 cm thick steaks
3 tablespoons roasted cashews
2 tablespoons coconut flakes,
    toasted if you like
¼ bunch of Thai basil, leaves picked

Preheat the oven to 180°C. Line a baking tray with baking paper.

Combine the coconut oil, soy sauce, vinegar, sriracha, coconut milk and 1 teaspoon of the paprika in a large mixing bowl. Add the cauliflower and coat the steaks generously. Pop the steaks onto the prepared tray and bake for 35–45 minutes until they are soft with some obvious signs of char (they should look a bit burnt).

Arrange the cauliflower steaks on a serving platter, sprinkle over the rest of the paprika and top with some extra sriracha (as much or as little as you like), the roasted cashews, coconut flakes and Thai basil leaves. Chow down.

HOW DO I COOK A STABLE RELATIONSHIP?

- Take two individuals
- Throw in half a bottle of tequila, some dancing and a touch of lust
- Turn up the heat
- Remove the regret
- Add laughter, banter, adventure and understanding
- Let it simmer away for a few weeks
- Now set aside and prepare 'the talk'
- If the two emulsify, then leave to ferment for a few more weeks
- Now, if all is well, they are trapped.

NOTE
DO NOT COAT WITH THE CRAY CRAY UNTIL AT LEAST 5 MONTHS IN

SIDE NOTE
I'M SINGLE

THAI GREEN CURRY

Okay, it's date night, but you've moved past the stage where you're cooking elaborate dishes with three elements plus a separate sauce and plating it beautifully, because, well, you've hidden your inner crazy for long enough now (I'm not speaking from experience or anything). But you still want to make something yum, something casual that still shows some care. This Thai curry is for those cosy nights in front of the TV, with a goblet of wine in hand and comfortably not talking to each other while you eat.

I find a lot of people are afraid to make their own curry paste. Everyone can make a green curry but people seem to shy away from the paste. I'm making it easy for you. A lot of the ingredients in this recipe you'll already have in your pantry; it may seem like a lot but that's what really rounds out the flavour. I've also upped the quantity because if you're gonna make green curry paste you might as well make enough to have on hand for your next five date nights. Also, you'll need the paste for my green curry prawn toast (page 162), which is legit the best brunch ever.

SERVES 2

1 tablespoon coconut oil
250 g skinless chicken breast, finely sliced
400 ml can coconut milk
250 ml (1 cup) chicken stock
1 zucchini, sliced
100 g broccoli florets
½ red capsicum, deseeded and chopped
100 g sugar snap peas, trimmed
2 teaspoons fish sauce
sea salt and freshly ground pepper
370 g (2 cups) cooked brown or wild rice
180 g (2 cups) bean sprouts
small handful of coriander leaves
sliced red chilli, to serve (optional)
2 tablespoons crushed Salted Peanuts (page 26)
2 lime wedges

GREEN CURRY PASTE

2 lemongrass stalks, white part only, roughly chopped
4 long green chillies, roughly chopped
2–6 Thai green chillies (depending on how hot you like it), roughly chopped
5 red shallots, roughly chopped
2 tablespoons grated galangal
7 cm piece of ginger, chopped
5 garlic cloves, chopped
3 coriander roots and stems, washed
6 makrut lime leaves (see page 13), chopped
2 teaspoons dried shrimp paste
2 tablespoons fish sauce
1 teaspoon grated fresh turmeric
1 teaspoon ground coriander
1 teaspoon ground cumin
¼ teaspoon ground white pepper
¼ teaspoon sea salt
2 teaspoons grated palm sugar
zest and juice of 1 lime, plus extra juice if needed
2–4 tablespoons coconut milk

TIPS: THIS GREEN CURRY PASTE RECIPE WILL MAKE ENOUGH PASTE FOR 25 CURRIES (I MIGHT BE EXAGGERATING ... IT'S MORE LIKE EIGHT CURRIES). WHAT I LIKE TO DO IS FREEZE THE LEFTOVER CURRY PASTE IN ICE-CUBE TRAYS AND THEN ZIP THEM INTO LITTLE PLASTIC BAGS FOR A LATER DATE (THEY WILL KEEP IN THE FREEZER FOR UP TO 2 MONTHS). OR YOU CAN POP THEM INTO LITTLE JARS AND GIFT THEM TO YOUR FRIENDS LIKE A PSYCHOPATH. (WHO GIVES PEOPLE CURRY PASTE? YOU NEED TO CALM DOWN. JUST BAKE THEM SOMETHING, LIKE MY STRAWBERRY BREAD ON PAGE 138.)

IF YOU WANT, YOU CAN SWAP OUT THE CHICKEN FOR PRAWNS — I DO IT ALL THE TIME. JUST COOK THE CURRY PASTE IN THE COCONUT OIL AND IGNORE THE CHICKEN BROWNING STEP, THEN POP THE PRAWNS INTO THE CURRY IN THE LAST 3 MINUTES OF COOKING.

To make the curry paste, process all the ingredients in a food processor (or blender or grinder — anything that chops, really) to form a paste, adding the coconut milk 1 tablespoon at a time just to make blending easier. Taste the paste — if it's too salty, add more lime; if you want more heat, add more chilli; if it's too hot, add more coconut milk. Set 3 tablespoons of the curry paste aside and see the Tips opposite for what to do with the rest.

Melt the coconut oil in a saucepan over high heat. Add the chicken and cook, stirring frequently, for 5–7 minutes until lightly browned. In goes the 3 tablespoons of curry paste. Cook for 2–3 minutes until fragrant, then add the coconut milk and stock. Reduce the heat to medium, cover and cook for 5 minutes.

Add the zucchini, broccoli, capsicum and sugar snap peas and simmer, uncovered, for 5 minutes. Finish by adding the fish sauce and simmer for 3 minutes. Add salt and pepper to taste.

Divide the rice into two deep bowls and spoon over the curry. Top with the bean sprouts, coriander and red chilli (if using). Sprinkle with the peanuts, pop a lime wedge in each bowl, snap a pic, upload to the gram with #couplegoals #foodporn and devour.

GREEN CURRY PRAWN TOAST with SRIRACHA MAYO

Prawn toast is an absolute banger of a dish: sweet prawn meat on crunchy bread with nutty sesame seeds. Yum. Can't get any better, right? That's what I thought, then one morning I was arguing to a guy I was seeing that you can't have green curry for breakfast (I was making green curry that night for our dinner). What happened next was life changing. You've probably guessed ... we kinda had green curry for breakfast because I'm a pushover. Well, we actually negotiated: I told him I'd use the green curry paste for a brekky dish, blitz it through some of the prawns I had ready for dinner and so this dish came into the world. Fragrant and aromatic curry paste paired with creamy and spicy sriracha mayo ... I can't. It is that good, you all just have to try it. It's sure to impress. Needless to say, I think he fell in love with me that day. (Side note: we don't talk anymore, but that doesn't have anything to do with the prawn toast.)

SERVES 4

400 g uncooked prawn meat
1 egg white
2½ teaspoons sesame oil
1 tablespoon Green Curry Paste (pages 160–1)
2 teaspoons caster sugar
pinch of sea salt
large pinch of ground white pepper
small handful of coriander sprigs, leaves picked and stems finely chopped
2 spring onions, white parts chopped and green parts cut into ribbons
4 slices of sourdough
3 tablespoons sesame seeds
neutral oil for deep-frying (such as vegetable oil)
1 tablespoon fried chilli strands (see Tip) or sliced red chilli

SRIRACHA MAYO
½ cup (125 g) 2-Minute Mayo (page 151)
1 tablespoon sriracha chilli sauce

To make the sriracha mayo, combine the ingredients in a small bowl.

In a food processor, combine the prawn meat, egg white, sesame oil, curry paste, sugar, salt, white pepper, coriander stem and chopped white spring onion. Pulse until it comes together into a rough paste. Refrigerate for 1 hour so that it firms up.

Using a butter knife, spread a 5 mm layer of prawn mixture onto each slice of bread, making sure you get right to the edges. Tip the sesame seeds onto a plate, then press the prawn side of the bread slices into the seeds to cover well.

Fill a large deep saucepan about one-third full with oil and heat to 180°C or until a cube of bread dropped in the oil browns in 15 seconds. Fry each slice of bread for 2–4 minutes, then flip and cook for a further 1–2 minutes until golden all over. Drain on paper towel.

If you want to impress, pop the sriracha mayo into a squeezy sauce bottle or piping bag fitted with a 1–2 mm nozzle and zigzag it over the toast (or you can just spoon it over if you don't have either of these). Top with the spring onion ribbons, coriander leaves (if using) and chilli.

TIP: FRIED CHILLI STRANDS ARE PIECES OF LONG CHILLIES THAT HAVE BEEN FINELY SLICED AND FRIED. THEY HAVE A MILD FLAVOUR AND ARE NOT VERY HOT. YOU CAN FIND THEM AT SPECIALTY FOOD STORES.

GREEN CURRY PRAWN
TOAST WITH SRIRACHA
MAYO (PAGE 162)

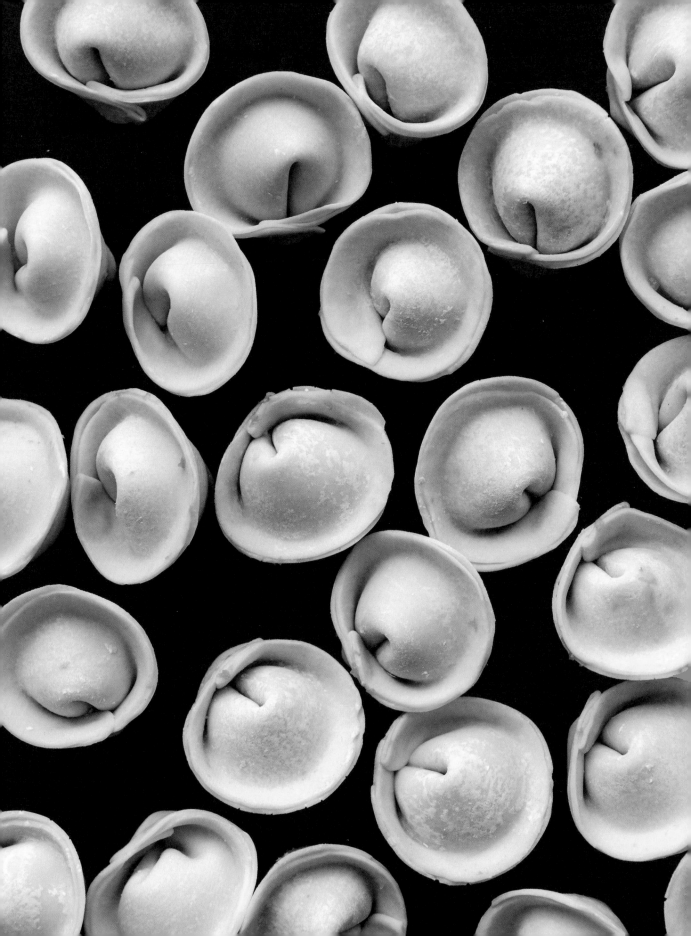

VEGEMITE AND CHICKEN DUMPLINGS (PAGE 168)

TIP: SERVE THESE DUMPLINGS WITH PEAS, TO GIVE A POP OF SWEETNESS AND FRESHNESS, OR WITH YOUR FAVOURITE PICKLES.

VEGEMITE and CHICKEN DUMPLINGS

Okay, I feel like this dish played a really weird part in my life. Let me explain. When I was on *MasterChef Australia* in 2018, it was a constant struggle for me at the beginning. I was confused all the time, I had no idea what the judges wanted and I'm pretty sure that they didn't know what to make of me. (Was I a DJ just there for the ride …? Well, no.) This dish won me an immunity pin and it really gave me the boost in confidence I needed at the time, so that's why it's here. I love my little Vegemite and chicken dumplings because they were a turning point in the competition for me.

SERVES 2

230 g skinless chicken thigh fillets,
    roughly chopped
sea salt
3 egg yolks
2 tablespoons double cream
1 teaspoon Vegemite
10 dumpling wrappers

BROTH
2 teaspoons vegetable oil
500 g chicken wings, chopped into
    2.5 cm pieces using a cleaver
2 red shallots, roughly chopped
1 carrot, diced
2 celery stalks, diced
6 cm piece of ginger, grated
1 long red chilli, finely diced
3 garlic cloves, crushed
1 litre (4 cups) chicken stock
1 tablespoon Vegemite
1 teaspoon fish sauce
sea salt

To make the broth, heat the vegetable oil in a saucepan over medium–high heat. Add the chicken wings and cook, turning occasionally, for 8–10 minutes until well browned all over. Add the shallot, carrot, celery, ginger, chilli and garlic and cook, stirring, for about 5 minutes until softened.

Pour in the chicken stock to deglaze the pan, scraping the base of the pan to release any yummy sticky bits. Add 400 ml of water and allow to simmer for 20 minutes. Strain the broth through a fine sieve into a clean saucepan, discarding the solids.

Place the strained broth over medium heat and simmer for about 10 minutes until reduced by half. Add the Vegemite and fish sauce and whisk until combined. Season with salt to taste. Set aside until you are ready to serve.

Meanwhile, to make the dumplings, place the chicken and a pinch of salt in a food processor and pulse until the chicken is finely chopped but not a paste. Add the egg yolks and pulse until combined. Add the cream and Vegemite and pulse until combined. Transfer to a piping bag. Pipe an equal-sized amount into the centre of each of the dumpling wrappers. Fold the wrappers over and seal the edges, using a little water if you need to (make sure you gently press out any air bubbles). Bring the two corners together and press to form a dumpling shape.

Bring a large saucepan of salted water to the boil. Add the dumplings and cook until they float to the surface (this should take about 3 minutes). Remove the dumplings with a slotted spoon and place in two serving bowls. Pour the broth over the dumplings and serve.

PICTURED ON PAGES 166–7

GRILLED OCCY and CRISPY CAPERS

My obsession with octopus started during a trip to Greece in 2018. I was in Athens for a friend's wedding and found myself ordering octopus in its grilled, charred, barbecued or marinated form whenever it was on the menu. I really fell in love with the sweetness of the octopus, which was always paired with something highly acidic. This is a dish to impress, great as an entree to share and oh-so easy. Octopus is one of those ingredients that could be scary to prepare, but nowadays you can buy it pre-tenderised from your fishmonger so there is no need to throw it against rocks like the Greeks do. Give this a try on your next date, it's also a great way to begin a conversation about Mykonos and what a beautiful country Greece is ...

SERVES 2

300 g tenderised octopus tentacles
2 tablespoons extra-virgin olive oil
2 teaspoons smoked paprika
zest and juice of 2 lemons
1 garlic clove, crushed
1 teaspoon onion powder
sea salt
handful of flat-leaf parsley leaves

CRISPY CAPERS
125 ml (½ cup) extra-virgin olive oil
3 tablespoons capers in brine,
    drained and patted dry
pinch of sea salt

Place the occy tentacles in a zip-lock bag with 1 tablespoon of the olive oil, 1 teaspoon of the paprika, the zest and juice of 1 lemon, the garlic, onion powder and a good pinch of salt. Squish the bag around so everything's mixed and the octopus is well coated, then leave to marinate for 15 minutes.

Heat a large griddle pan over high heat and cook the octopus for 3–5 minutes on each side until it is nice and charred. Set aside to rest.

To make the crispy capers, heat the olive oil in a small saucepan over high heat to 180°C or until a cube of bread dropped in the oil browns in 15 seconds. Add the capers and fry for 30–60 seconds until the capers have browned and puffed open. Be careful because they will pop. Transfer to paper towel to drain, then sprinkle with the salt.

Slice the occy into pieces and arrange on a serving plate. Spoon the crispy capers over the top, then finish with the remaining olive oil, lemon juice and zest and paprika and sprinkle with the parsley and some salt.

PICTURED ON PAGES 170–1

GRiLLED OCCY AND CRiSPY CAPERS

(PAGE 169)

CRISPY PORK BELLY and RIBBON SALAD

Crispy pork belly is my go-to dish when I want to impress with minimal effort. I know that sounds unbelievable but stay with me: this pork belly is foolproof. This recipe came about when I wanted to cook for a boyfriend, Brad (you know, the one who ended up cheating on me). He was coeliac and I was stressing about making something he could have on our first actual 'me at home cooking' date. Isn't it funny the pressure we put on ourselves when we want to impress a potential partner? You can trust me when I say this dish isn't as complicated as it looks. When it comes to your date, however, I can't make any promises.

SERVES 2

500 g boneless pork belly
2 tablespoons sea salt
3 teaspoons five-spice powder
80 ml (⅓ cup) hoisin sauce

RIBBON SALAD

1 cucumber, cut into ribbons using a peeler
1 carrot, cut into ribbons using a peeler
4 radishes, finely sliced
small handful of coriander leaves
small handful of Vietnamese mint leaves
small handful of mint leaves
3 tablespoons Nuoc Mam Dipping Sauce (page 34)

Preheat the oven to 200°C.

Score the skin of the pork in a criss-cross pattern at 1 cm intervals. Place on a baking tray, then rub the skin with 2 teaspoons of the salt. Leave to sweat in the fridge for 15 minutes.

Use paper towel to dab the moisture off the pork skin, then rub the remaining salt over the skin again. Rub the five-spice onto all the meaty parts of the pork, leaving the skin.

Place in the oven for 40–50 minutes, then increase the heat to 250°C and cook for a further 15–20 minutes until the skin is puffed and deep brown. Remove and rest for 15 minutes.

While your pork is resting, make the ribbon salad. This one is super easy – all you have to do is mix everything in a large bowl.

Cut the pork belly in half. Smear some hoisin sauce onto two serving plates, place a piece of pork on top, then arrange the ribbon salad on the side. Serve immediately.

SHAKING BEEF

This is possibly the most popular dish on the menu at my restaurant, The George on Collins. If my friends are dining, I always recommend they order this – the smell of the beef totally captivates and mesmerises the room as it comes out of the kitchen. It's the perfect dish for a date. When you're making this, remember to prep everything but leave the actual cooking for when your date or partner has arrived. The name itself hints at how the beef is cooked – jumping, skipping and shaking away in your wok to ensure beautiful charry caramelisation on the outside and soft, sweet, rare beef on the inside. The beef is a flavour bomb which contrasts with the peppery green watercress and hits of acidity from the tomato and vinegar onion that really lift the dish. Pop this recipe onto your must-make list. I've cooked it for three different partners, all of whom asked for it on the reg.

SERVES 4

600 g eye or scotch fillet, cut into 2.5 cm cubes
4 garlic cloves, crushed
3 tablespoons vegetable oil
3 tablespoons oyster sauce
2 tablespoons dark soy sauce
1 tablespoon caster sugar
sea salt and freshly ground black pepper
1 red capsicum, deseeded and cut into 2.5 cm pieces
200 g watercress
1 large tomato, finely sliced

VINEGAR RED ONION
1 red onion, finely sliced
2 tablespoons caster sugar
80 ml (⅓ cup) white vinegar

DIPPING SAUCE
2 teaspoons sea salt
2 teaspoons freshly ground black pepper
juice of 1 large lemon

Place the beef in a large mixing bowl with half the garlic. Add 1 tablespoon of the vegetable oil, the oyster sauce, soy sauce, sugar, a pinch of salt and 1 teaspoon of pepper and combine well. Leave to marinate for at least 30 minutes.

To make the vinegar red onion (basically a quick pickle), combine the ingredients in a non-reactive bowl and leave for 15 minutes.

Next, make your dipping sauce by combining the ingredients in a bowl. Set aside.

Place a wok over high heat. Add 1 tablespoon of the remaining oil and heat until just before smoking point. Add half of the remaining garlic and leave to slightly brown for 5 seconds. Add half the marinated beef and leave to brown while gently shaking the pan in intervals for 2–3 minutes. Add half the capsicum in the last 15 seconds.

Remove the cooked beef and capsicum and set aside. Heat the remaining oil in the wok and repeat with the remaining garlic, beef and capsicum.

To serve, place the watercress on a platter and top with the cooked beef. Drain the vinegar red onion and arrange it next to the beef, along with the sliced tomato. Finish with some freshly ground pepper and serve with the dipping sauce.

TIP: THIS RECIPE MAKES ENOUGH FOR FOUR SERVES BECAUSE I LIKE TO COOK HALF THE BEEF AND KEEP THE REMAINDER MARINATING TO COOK AGAIN FOR DINNER THE FOLLOWING NIGHT. THE WONDERFUL SAUCE ACTS LIKE A KIND OF BRINE FOR THE BEEF AND MAKES IT SO MUCH MORE TENDER.

WHAT'S YOUR IDEAL SATURDAY NIGHT DINNER?

- Mediterranean
- 6'1"+
- Cheeky smile
- Bronzed
- Fit but enjoys carbs
- Good teeth
- Strong enough to throw me through a wall

And ...
- Tequila

SEXY CHOCOLATE COMB

Chocolate comb has been playing on my mind for a very long time. The thought process being, there are plenty of recipes for honeycomb dipped in chocolate (which is bomb) but I'd never been able to find a recipe for chocolate-flavoured honeycomb. After spending some time tweaking and burning about half a dozen batches I have finally made what I am after. This recipe is like a little science experiment – with quite precise measurements – the bicarb soda makes the liquid foam up, increase in size and bubble away as it cools.

SERVES 8

10 g cocoa powder
8 g bicarbonate of soda
150 g caster sugar
65 g glucose syrup
25 g honey

Line a deep heatproof bowl with two sheets of baking paper so the paper is sticking up around the side. I find that scrunching the baking paper first really helps it stay in the bowl.

Sift the cocoa powder and bicarb soda together into a small bowl so it's all ready for your chemical reaction. Place the sugar, glucose, honey and 1½ tablespoons of water in a non-reactive saucepan and place over high heat. Pop a kitchen thermometer in and watch it carefully (without stirring) as the mixture heats to 154°C. This should take 7–10 minutes. Once it hits 154°C, quickly turn off the heat, whisk in the cocoa and bicarb mixture (watch out, as the bicarb will make the mixture foam up), then carefully pour into the prepared bowl.

Let the chocolate comb sit undisturbed for at least 40 minutes, remembering not to move it during that time or you may knock the all-important bubbles out. Once fully cooled and solidified I like to use the back of a knife to break it into shards, either bite-sized or larger depending on if you are using the chocolate comb as a treat on its own or as decoration for a cake or pavlova.

The comb will keep in an airtight container for up to 1 week but it will start to lose its crunchiness after a couple of days. Don't keep it in the fridge.

CHOOSE-YOUR-OWN ICE CREAM

If you've ever wondered why contestants make so much ice cream on *MasterChef*, it's because we all have our own base recipe and changing the flavour is very easy. This is the base that I use, and I know a few people reading this will be surprised by the use of whole eggs, but I swear by this recipe. Once you have the base mastered, have some fun trying different flavours by infusing the liquid first or simply adding spices to the mixture.

MAKES 1 LITRE

500 ml (2 cups) thickened cream
300 ml full-cream milk
2 eggs, plus 3 yolks
150 g caster sugar
pinch of sea salt

TIP: THIS RECIPE IS GREAT FOR INFUSING WITH DIFFERENT FLAVOURS. THINK LEMONGRASS, BAY LEAVES, CITRUS ZEST, GINGER AND A LOAD OF OTHER SPICES. ALL YOU HAVE TO DO IS PLACE YOUR INGREDIENT OF CHOICE INTO THE CREAM AND MILK AT THE BEGINNING. LEAVE TO INFUSE FOR 15 MINUTES, THEN FOLLOW THE REST OF THE RECIPE, DISCARDING ANY SOLIDS BEFORE ADDING TO THE EGG MIXTURE.

Combine the cream and milk in a saucepan and bring to a simmer over low heat.

Place the eggs and egg yolks in the bowl of a stand mixer fitted with the whisk attachment, add the sugar and salt and beat for 2–4 minutes on high until pale and creamy. Turn the mixer to low and gradually add the hot cream mixture, beating until combined.

Wipe out the saucepan. Return the mixture to the pan and place over medium heat. Cook, stirring gently with a silicone spatula, until the mixture thickens and reaches 83°C on a kitchen thermometer. Remove from the heat and strain into a bowl set over an ice bath to cool. Once cold, transfer to an ice cream machine and churn according to the manufacturer's instructions. Place in the freezer to set before serving.

CHOOSE YOUR FLAVOUR!

VANiLLA

Add 2 teaspoons of vanilla bean paste to the cream and milk mixture at the beginning.

PEANUT BUTTER

Add 3 tablespoons of peanut butter to the cream and milk mixture at the beginning.

CiNNAMON

Add 1 teaspoon of ground cinnamon and 1 cinnamon stick to the cream and milk mixture at the beginning. Leave to infuse over low heat for 15 minutes. Discard the stick before adding to the egg mixture.

HONEY

Add 80 ml (⅓ cup) of honey to the cream and milk mixture at the beginning. Reduce the amount of sugar by 50 g.

MY DRUNK and STICKY DATE

My drunk and sticky date pudding was the first sweet dish I made on *MasterChef* that was a success. Before that, I was terrified of making desserts. It now lives happily as a must-have on the menu at my restaurant and I have no plans to take it off. This recipe is perfect for date night because it always impresses, the warmth from the cinnamon and whisky singing to each other in great harmony. Prepare for your date to salivate while watching the whisky caramel being poured over the puddings. Always serve with a good-quality vanilla ice cream. I can't even describe how delicious this actually is, you'll just have to make it.

SERVES 2 GENEROUSLY

100 g pitted dates, chopped
1 teaspoon bicarbonate of soda
150 ml boiling water
100 g brown sugar
50 g softened butter, plus extra
    for greasing
1 large egg
1 teaspoon vanilla bean paste
100 g (⅔ cup) plain flour, sifted
1 teaspoon ground cinnamon
pinch of sea salt
vanilla ice cream, to serve

WHISKY CARAMEL
200 ml cream
80 ml (⅓ cup) whisky
½ teaspoon sea salt
200 g caster sugar
40 g salted butter

Preheat the oven to 180°C. Grease six 125 ml dariole moulds or ramekins with butter.

Place the dates, bicarb soda and boiling water in a large bowl, give it a little stir and leave to soften for 5 minutes.

In the bowl of a stand mixer fitted with the whisk attachment, beat the brown sugar and butter until pale and light. Add the egg and vanilla and mix well. Now in goes the flour, cinnamon and salt. Mix until smooth. Add the dates and soaking liquid and mix until combined (it will look lumpy because of the dates – this is fine).

Fill your moulds to two-thirds full with the batter, then place on a tray and pop in the oven for 16–20 minutes until a skewer inserted into the centre comes out clean. Set aside to cool for 10 minutes.

While your puddings are cooking, make your whisky caramel. In a small saucepan over medium heat, warm the cream, whisky and salt. Place the sugar in another small saucepan over medium heat and cook for 6–9 minutes until melted and caramelised (it should turn deep amber in colour). Pour the cream mixture into the caramel (it will bubble – that's cool, chill). Add the butter and cook, stirring, for 5 minutes.

Remove the puddings from their moulds and tear them into big chunks onto two serving plates. Pour as much whisky caramel as you want over the top and serve with vanilla ice cream, because you're worth it.

CHAPTER FIVE

BEING BASIC

SIMPLE AND HEALTHY EATS
FOR EVERY DAY

Being basic is exactly as it sounds – basic recipes we should all know. To me, the dishes in this chapter are about self-care, staying healthy-ish and having recipes that are easily adaptable up your sleeve.

It's your 'day in, day out' chapter – great for food prepping with ingredients that I have readily available in the pantry and that I think you'll probably have in yours, too. There are simple breakfasts, tasty but fuss-free lunches, healthy snacks and quick dinners.

This chapter is all about looking after yourself, embracing cooking as part of your routine and keeping food fun but also not over-complicating things. I share dishes that I may not put on the gram but that I eat multiple times a week, and I tackle that end-of-week veg we all seem to have left in the fridge so that nothing goes to waste. I will also introduce you to some of my staples, my old and new loves.

Some people think that being basic is a negative thing, but I say let's embrace it! I'm proud to be basic because sometimes the best things in life are just that.

Whether you choose the five different ways to jazz up a vermicelli noodle salad (pages 213–20) or the eggs I have every morning (page 188), I hope you have fun cooking these recipes, because food should always be enjoyable. It's time to show yourself some love, to be your own motivation and your own hero.

BASIC!

WHAT'S IN THIS CHAPTER?

♡ RICE PAPER ROLLS WITH INGREDIENTS YOU CAN INTERCHANGE FOR A QUICK AND HEALTHY LUNCH OR DINNER (PAGES 200–1).

♡ EGGS YOU POP ON BEFORE YOUR POST-GYM SHOWER THAT WILL COOK WHILE YOU SORT YOUR SHIT OUT FOR THE DAY (PAGE 188).

♡ FRIED RICE THAT IS LOADED FULL OF DELICIOUS VEG AND TASTES EVEN BETTER FOR TOMORROW'S LUNCH (PAGE 195).

♡ THE PERFECT 3 PM PICK-ME-UP SNACK THAT YOU CAN MAKE IN BULK AT THE BEGINNING OF THE WEEK (PAGE 222).

♡ THE EASIEST EVER FRIED CHICKEN THAT YOU CAN HAVE ON HAND IN THE FREEZER AT ALL TIMES (PAGE 206).

POST-GYM EGGS

TBH, most people know how to make an omelette, but what I didn't know until my late teens is that not everyone makes an omelette with soy sauce, ginger and shallots. This omelette is perfect for when you're in a rush because of how it is cooked. Most mornings I either go to the gym or pilates and then come home to get ready for my day. With this recipe, I can prep and begin cooking the eggs as soon as I get home, then I pop a lid on and turn off the heat so the residual heat cooks the eggs while I shower. Once I'm done, so are the eggs!

SERVES 2

3 eggs
3 tablespoons full-cream milk
1 teaspoon onion powder
pinch of sea salt
1 tablespoon light soy sauce
2 tablespoons extra-virgin olive oil
¼ red capsicum, deseeded
   and diced
1 garlic clove, finely chopped
1 small red shallot, finely chopped
1 spring onion, finely chopped
4 cm piece of ginger, finely chopped
½ long red chilli, finely chopped
2 tablespoons grated pecorino
1 tablespoon crispy fried shallots
freshly ground black pepper
small handful of pea tendrils
   (see Tip)

In a small bowl, whisk the eggs, milk, onion powder, salt and soy sauce and set aside.

Heat 1 tablespoon of the olive oil in a small non-stick frying pan over medium heat. Add the capsicum, garlic, shallot, spring onion, ginger and chilli. You'll want to cook these for 2–3 minutes until softened, then remove from the pan (usually I just pop the mixture back on my wooden chopping board).

Reduce the heat to low, add the remaining olive oil to the pan and pour in the egg mixture. Cook for 2–3 minutes until about half cooked, pulling the egg mixture in towards the centre of the pan about every 15 seconds with a silicone spatula. Spoon the veggies onto the egg then top with the pecorino. Cover with a lid and cook for 2–3 minutes until the cheese has melted, or you can cover, turn off the heat and leave for 8–10 minutes and let the residual heat fully cook the eggs.

Sprinkle the crispy shallots over the omelette followed by a generous amount of black pepper, top with the pea tendrils and eat right out of the pan with a mate (well, that's what my housemate Diana and I do, anyway).

TIP: IF YOU CAN'T BUY PEA TENDRILS, IT'S FINE TO USE WHATEVER LEAFY GREENS YOU CAN FIND. I'VE TOPPED MINE WITH SPINACH, KALE AND ROCKET IN THE PAST.

SMASHED AVO and POACHIES

Smashed avo is such an Aussie staple, yet so many of us don't make it at home. I literally eye roll whenever my friends order smashed avo at brunch (that may be the inner cheapskate in me). Why not spend five bucks a serve at home rather than nineteen plus at your local cafe? This dish is a breakfast fave of mine and I make it for friends, family, my housemate Diana and even some lucky dates. It's very easy and I usually have most of the ingredients on hand in the pantry. Don't be afraid to poach the eggs (just don't move the water). Crunchy bread, creamy avo and oozy eggs ... HEAVEN.

SERVES 2

1 avocado, diced
2 cubes of good-quality marinated goat's cheese, plus 1 teaspoon of the oil
¼ bunch of coriander, leaves and stems finely chopped
½ teaspoon ground cumin
sea salt
4 eggs
2 slices of good-quality bread (multigrain or sourdough), toasted
¼ teaspoon cumin seeds, toasted
microherbs, to serve (optional)
lemon wedges, to serve

Combine the avocado, goat's cheese and oil, chopped coriander leaves and stalks, ground cumin and ¼ teaspoon of salt in a bowl. Use a fork to gently mash the ingredients without overworking the avocado or goat's cheese. Set aside.

Bring a large saucepan of water to a low simmer, crack two eggs into two ramekins or small dishes. Turn the heat down to just below a simmer and gently lower the ramekins into the water and let the eggs slide in. Cook the eggs for 1 minute, then, using a slotted spoon, wiggle them off the bottom of the pan once the whites are cooked enough to hold together. Cook for a further minute, then remove the eggs onto a plate lined with paper towel. Repeat the process with the remaining two eggs (remember not to stir the water).

Place the toast on a couple of plates. Spread the avo on your toast and top each with two poachies. Sprinkle with the cumin seeds and microherbs (if you want to be a bit fancy), and finish with a pinch of salt. Serve with lemon wedges on the side.

THE BEST WAY TO DRINK WATER?

- Mix ½ glass of cold water with ice and 50 ml of vodka.
- Top with fresh lime juice.
- Warning: If you do this too often it may result in texts to your ex, sudden bursts of confidence or eruptions of Ariana Grande songs while dancing on tables.

YOUR NEW FAVOURITE CHARRED CABBAGE

Cabbage has been my obsession for a while now, it's such a versatile veggie. My favourite is the sugarloaf cabbage as it's naturally sweet and so full of flavour. Like other veggies in the brassica family, such as brussels sprouts, cabbage loves being charred. The caramelisation helps it release its natural sweetness. I like to take it right up to the point where it's almost burnt. I make this every couple of weeks for friends and family, converting everyone into cabbage lovers, one burnt leaf at a time.

SERVES 2

- 1 tablespoon neutral oil (such as grapeseed)
- ½ sugarloaf cabbage or ½ small savoy cabbage, cut into thick wedges
- 3 tablespoons unsalted butter, plus extra if needed
- 3 tablespoons Chimichurri (page 126)
- 80 g (¾ cup) toasted walnuts, roughly chopped

Heat the oil in a large heavy-based frying pan over high heat. Pop in the cabbage, cut-side down, and leave to cook undisturbed for 8–10 minutes – the bottom of the cabbage should be nice and charred and almost black. Flip the cabbage over and cook on the other side for 3 minutes.

Add the butter, reduce the heat to medium and cook for 3–4 minutes. At this point the butter should have been bubbling for a good couple of minutes, so it's time to baste the cabbage. Tilt the pan towards you and spoon the butter onto the cabbage. Cook for 2 minutes, tilting and spooning the butter over the cabbage every 15 seconds or so. The butter should be getting browner and nuttier. If you think the butter is getting too dark, add an extra tablespoon to bring it back. Now leave the cabbage to cook undisturbed for a further 2–3 minutes or until the bottom is completely charred.

Place the cabbage on a serving plate and spoon some of the pan juices over. Top with the chimichurri and scatter over the walnuts. Trust me, you'll never look at cabbage the same way again.

HEALTHY FRIED 'RICE'

Every cook should have a fried rice recipe, and here I've subbed out the rice for cauliflower to make it healthier. I usually make this on food prep days as a simple dish that's easily stored and reheated, and it's so tasty. You can just throw in any veg you have on hand, such as green beans, asparagus and even chickpeas. It's an 'anything goes' kinda dish because most of the flavour comes from the eggs and sausage and the sauces you finish with.

SERVES 4

400 g cauliflower, florets and
    stalk roughly chopped
3 eggs
2 tablespoons full-cream milk
1 tablespoon soy sauce
sea salt
1 tablespoon vegetable oil
2 lap cheong (Chinese sausage),
    finely diced
1 teaspoon sesame oil
1 large head of broccoli, finely
    chopped
1 carrot, finely diced
225 g (1½ cups) frozen peas
    and corn
2 teaspoons caster sugar (optional)
1½ tablespoons kecap manis

Place the cauliflower in a food processor and pulse into small pieces about the size of rice.

Beat the eggs and milk with 1 teaspoon of the soy sauce and a pinch of salt in a mixing bowl.

Get a wok nice and hot over high heat. Add the vegetable oil and pour the egg mixture in – the egg should start cooking straight away. Gently tilt the wok in all directions to spread out the egg to make a nice thin omelette and cook for 1 minute. Pull the edge of the omelette inwards using a silicone spatula and tilt the wok around again so that any uncooked egg coats the side of the wok. Cook for 2 minutes, then flip the omelette and cook for another 2 minutes. Remove, set aside to cool, then dice the omelette into 1 cm pieces. Set aside for later.

Meanwhile, wipe out the wok and return to high heat. Add the lap cheong and sesame oil and cook for 3 minutes. Reduce the heat to medium and add the broccoli and carrot. Cook, stirring, for 2–3 minutes, until the carrot softens. Add the cauliflower rice and cook for 4–6 minutes until the cauliflower has softened. Add the corn and peas and the sugar (if using) and cook for 2 minutes or until the contents of the wok have begun to dry and caramelise. Turn the heat back to high, pour in the kecap manis and the remaining soy sauce, mix well and cook for 2 minutes, keeping everything moving, to fully dry out the fried 'rice'. Serve into bowls and enjoy.

END-OF-THE-WEEK ROAST VEG

At the end of every week I always have random vegetables left over in my fridge or pantry that I need to use up before my next big market shop. Never knowing what to do with them, I started roasting whatever I had to have a healthy meal or two ready to go whenever I needed a refuel. The best thing about this is that it changes from week to week based on your leftovers. I also change up my herbs and sometimes add spices such as cumin and sumac or even a little dukkah or other premade spice mixes. It's a massive choose your own adventure and it cuts down on food wastage. Plus roast veg is always delicious!

SERVES 4

2 carrots, cut into 5 cm pieces
2 beetroot, each cut into 8 wedges
1 sweet potato, cut into 2 cm thick rounds
100 g (1 cup) brussels sprouts, halved
¼ head of cauliflower, cut into bite-sized pieces
1 fennel bulb, cut into 8 wedges
1 red onion, cut into wedges
1 head of garlic, halved crossways
1–2 tablespoons extra-virgin olive oil
generous pinch of sea salt
sprigs of rosemary, thyme or oregano (optional)

Preheat the oven to 200°C. Line two large baking trays with baking paper.

Place the carrot, beetroot and sweet potato on one prepared tray, then place the brussels sprouts, cauliflower and fennel on the other tray. Split the onion and garlic between the two trays, drizzle with the oil and sprinkle over the salt and some herbs, if you like. The reason we split the vegetables up is that hardier veg such as carrot, beetroot, potato, sweet potato, celeriac and pumpkin take longer to roast (30–45 minutes) than more delicate veg like brussels sprouts, cauliflower, fennel, broccoli and cabbage, which usually take 20–30 minutes.

So, with that in mind, first pop the tray with the carrot into the oven for 10 minutes, then pop the other tray in and leave both to roast away for 20–30 minutes, checking until they're cooked to your desired softness.

Store your roast veg in an airtight container in the fridge for up to 4 days. Use as a base for salads, serve on the side of grilled meat or fish, or add to your morning omelette or scrambled eggs.

MILLENNIAL CHICKEN SALAD

This salad is one I often take with me on hikes and picnics, plus it's great for lunches. I feel like raw broccoli is seriously underappreciated and should be used more, because it's so delicious and sweet. And when the avocado is perfectly ripe, it creates a kind of dressing with the lemon juice and goat's cheese. The pistachios give this dish a distinct and captivating crunch and nuttiness, which makes it oh-so moreish. I call this my millennial chicken salad because it contains all the things we millennials love: avocado, pistachio, buckwheat, goat's cheese and raw broccoli, because #cleaneating.

SERVES 2

100 g (½ cup) buckwheat
1 head of broccoli
juice of 1 lemon
1 avocado, diced
60 g shelled pistachios, chopped
1 long red chilli, sliced
½ roast chicken, meat picked
  and chopped
50 g goat's cheese, crumbled
pinch of sea salt

Cook the buckwheat according to the packet instructions, give it a fluff with a fork and allow to cool completely.

Shred the broccoli florets using either a knife or a box grater. Pop them in a large bowl and douse with the lemon juice.

Throw in the cooled buckwheat, along with all the remaining ingredients. Toss well and serve.

3 BASIC AF RICE PAPER ROLLS

Interactive foods are my favourite. Think tacos, grazing platters and hotpots. Rice paper rolls, I feel, are another dish everyone needs to add to their DIY repertoire. Super healthy, simple and fun, also perfect to pre-roll and pack away for lunch the next day. I sometimes make them, slice them up and serve them as canapes, too. If you're having these for dinner, put all the ingredients out on your table with a bowl of hot water and roll as you go. The secret to a truly great rice paper roll is to load them up with herbs. Don't rip a single mint leaf into pieces, throw four whole leaves in – you want that punch of flavour to the face.

SERVES 2

RICE PAPER ROLLS with PRAWN and PORK

sea salt
150 g boneless pork belly
100 g raw king prawns
Nuoc Mam Dipping Sauce (page 34)
8 rice paper sheets
150 g cooked vermicelli noodles
1 bunch of mustard greens, chopped
1 carrot, cut into matchsticks
1 cucumber, cut into matchsticks
1 bunch of mint, leaves picked
1 bunch of Vietnamese mint,
    leaves picked
1 bunch of coriander, leaves picked
1 bunch of garlic chives (optional)

Fill a saucepan with water and add 1 teaspoon of salt. Bring to the boil over medium–high heat. Add the pork belly and poach for 13–16 minutes until the liquid runs clear when the pork is pierced with a knife. Remove the pork with a slotted spoon (you'll reuse the water to poach the prawns) and plunge into an ice bath. Drain and finely slice, then transfer to a small plate.

Add the prawns to the saucepan and poach for 2–3 minutes until the prawns are firm and a nice orange and white colour. Drain and plunge the prawns into another ice bath. Drain again, peel and devein the prawns, then slice in half lengthways and transfer to a small plate.

Pour the nuoc mam into two little dipping bowls (so you don't have to share) to serve with the rice paper rolls.

To assemble, dip a sheet of rice paper in hot water to soften and then place on a plate. Pop some halved prawns horizontally near the middle of the rice paper (a bit closer to you than the middle). Top with some pork, noodles, vegetables, mint and coriander. Now to roll, fold in the sides of the rice paper so the ingredients fit snugly. If you want to get a bit fancy, pop a few garlic chives in now, so that they stick out of one end of the roll. Then, starting from the edge closest to you, roll it tightly all the way up. Dip in the nuoc mam and eat and repeat.

PICTURED ON PAGES 202–3

VEGAN RAINBOW RICE PAPER ROLLS

8 rice paper sheets
1 carrot, grated
½ avocado, cut into strips
150 g cooked vermicelli noodles
¼ red cabbage, finely sliced
250 g firm tofu, sliced into 8 strips
1 cucumber, cut into matchsticks
½ bunch of Vietnamese mint,
    leaves picked
½ bunch of mint, leaves picked

PEANUT DIPPING SAUCE
3 tablespoons peanut butter
3 tablespoons light soy sauce
2 tablespoons sriracha chilli sauce
juice and zest of 1 lime
1 tablespoon hoisin sauce
2 tablespoons crushed Salted
    Peanuts (page 26)

To make the dipping sauce, just pop all the ingredients in a mixing bowl and whisk until combined. Pour into two little dipping bowls (so you don't have to share) to serve with the rice paper rolls.

To assemble, dip a sheet of rice paper in hot water to soften and then place on a plate. Pop a little line of carrot horizontally near the middle of the rice paper (a bit closer to you than the middle). Top with a strip of avocado, then some noodles, cabbage, tofu, cucumber and herbs. Now to roll, fold in the sides of the rice paper so the ingredients fit snugly, then, starting from the edge closest to you, roll it tightly all the way up. Dip in the sauce and eat and repeat.

TUNA and WASABI PONZU RICE PAPER ROLLS

8 rice paper sheets
16 shiso leaves
½ avocado, cut into strips
1 cucumber, cut into matchsticks
2 tablespoons furikake (see Tip
    page 74)
250 g sashimi-grade tuna, sliced
    into 8 strips
150 g cooked vermicelli noodles
1 bunch of coriander, leaves picked

WASABI PONZU DIPPING SAUCE
1 tablespoon wasabi paste
3 tablespoons light soy sauce
3 tablespoons rice wine vinegar
3 tablespoons orange juice
2 teaspoons finely grated
    orange zest
1½ tablespoons warmed honey
2 teaspoons grated ginger

To make the dipping sauce, just pop all the ingredients in a mixing bowl and whisk until combined. Pour into two little dipping bowls (so you don't have to share) to serve with the rice paper rolls.

To assemble, dip a sheet of rice paper in hot water to soften and then place on a plate. Place two shiso leaves in a line horizontally near the middle of the rice paper (a bit closer to you than the middle) and lay a strip of avocado and some cucumber on top. Sprinkle 1 teaspoon of furikake onto the rice paper above the shiso and top that with a strip of tuna and some noodles and coriander. Now to roll, fold in the sides of the rice paper so the ingredients fit snugly, then, starting from the edge closest to you, roll it tightly all the way up. Dip in the sauce and eat and repeat.

PLUMP AF!

RICE PAPER ROLLS
WITH PRAWN AND PORK
(PAGE 200)

FRESH

(KINDA) GREEK SALAD

Okay. REAL. TALK. You know how you generally have tomatoes, cucumbers and capsicums in the house, no matter what? Well, this is my 'go-to lunch when I have nothing' recipe. By adding just a few more staples, you end up with such a banging meal. The shining star of this dish is the combination of oregano and good-quality olive oil (which, plus the feta, is what makes the salad kinda Greek). The proteins are always negotiable, for me it's whatever I've got hanging in the fridge or pantry for 'rainy days' – rainy days being my way of saying when I CBF cooking – so feel free to switch out the tuna, cheese and/or walnuts for whatever you have on hand. Try this with soft-boiled eggs or leftover roast chicken.

SERVES 1

1 large tomato, cut into 1 cm pieces
1 small Lebanese cucumber, cut into 1 cm pieces
½ red capsicum, deseeded and cut into 1 cm pieces
40 g feta
85 g can tuna in chilli oil, drained and oil reserved
1 teaspoon good-quality extra-virgin olive oil
juice of ½ lemon
1 teaspoon dried oregano (see Tip)
pinch of sea salt
40 g walnuts, roughly chopped
1 soft-boiled egg, halved
freshly ground black pepper

In a large mixing bowl, combine the tomato, cucumber and capsicum. Crumble in the feta and flake the tuna over the top.

Mix the drained tuna oil with the olive oil, lemon juice, oregano and salt. Pour the dressing over the salad and toss to combine.

Transfer to a plate, top with the walnuts, egg and some freshly ground pepper and eat up.

TIP: OREGANO IS VERY IMPORTANT IN THIS DISH. I ALWAYS GET MY OREGANO DRIED ON THE STEM FROM THE MARKET AND CRUMBLE IT MYSELF. THE FLAVOUR IS SO MUCH BETTER THAN THE DRIED OREGANO YOU GET IN THE LITTLE SPICE SHAKERS.

THE EASIEST FRIED CHICKEN EVER

You will never need another fried chicken recipe again. I have no idea how this one came about but it's been my go-to for years. It's uber crispy and crunchy – perfect for those lazy days (maybe when you're hungover) when all you want is fried chicken. I call this a basic because, well … everyone needs a fried chicken recipe. Funny story: I made this once when I was still in high school, but the oil was way too hot and I basically caused an oil fire in my aunt's house. It's okay, everyone survived. The chicken ribs didn't, though … so sad. Moral of that story? Always check your oil temperature when deep-frying because, you know, safety first.

SERVES 2-4

1 kg skin-on chicken ribs (you can sub with chicken winglets but your butcher will defs have ribs)
neutral oil for deep-frying (such as vegetable oil)
2-Minute Mayo (page 151), to serve (optional)

SUPER-SIMPLE SEASONING
2 tablespoons chicken stock powder
1 teaspoon freshly ground black pepper
150 g cornflour
large pinch of sea salt

This one's an easy one, all you do is place all the seasoning ingredients in a large zip-lock bag, add the chicken, give it all a good shake and leave in the fridge for 1 hour.

Remove the chicken from the fridge 20 minutes before you want to cook, to bring it to room temperature.

Half-fill a saucepan with oil and place over medium heat to bring it to 180°C or until a cube of bread dropped in the oil browns in 15 seconds.

Fry the chicken in batches for 8–12 minutes until golden and crispy. Remove using a slotted spoon and place on paper towel to drain.

Serve this chicken with absolutely nothing because it is delicious just the way it is … Okay, if you want mayo, go for it.

TIP: I ALWAYS HAVE A FEW ZIP-LOCK BAGS OF THIS CHICKEN IN MY FREEZER, READY TO GO FOR ANY TIME I HAVE TO ENTERTAIN ON SHORT NOTICE. IT WILL KEEP FOR A COUPLE OF MONTHS, BUT MINE NEVER LASTS THAT LONG. JUST DEFROST AND FRY — SO EASY.

CRISPY FISH TACOS

My close friends know that I have an obsession with Mexican and Tex-Mex food. It all came about on a trip to Cabo with a detour to LA in 2015. The way the Mexican flavours are pounded into every dish, with high levels of acidity and different textures? Delish! Everyone should have a taco recipe up their sleeve and mine is all about the crispy fish and the fresh salsa.

P.S. This is a great dish to pull out on taco Tuesdays as it always impresses.

SERVES 2

60 g plain flour
1 teaspoon smoked paprika
1 teaspoon ground cumin
1 teaspoon garlic powder
pinch of sea salt
2 eggs, lightly beaten
120 g (2 cups) panko breadcrumbs
250 g barramundi or other firm, white fish fillets, cut into strips
neutral oil for deep-frying (such as vegetable oil)
6 soft corn or wheat tortilla, warmed (or you can use hard taco shells if you prefer)
¼ red cabbage, shredded
1 baby cos lettuce, shredded

SMOKED MAYO
3 tablespoons 2-Minute Mayo (page 151)
1 teaspoon smoked paprika
juice and zest of 1 lime
pinch of sea salt

SALSA
1 red shallot, finely diced
1 long red chilli, finely sliced
1 garlic clove, crushed
1 tomato, deseeded and chopped
1 avocado, diced
1 teaspoon sea salt
juice of ½ lime
1 teaspoon ground cumin
small handful of coriander leaves, roughly chopped

To make the smoked mayo, place all the ingredients in a small bowl, mix well and set aside.

Next, make your salsa. (I feel like every time we make something this simple I have to bulk out the method because I assume everyone knows how to slice and dice.) Anyway, place all the ingredients in a bowl and mix using a fork to gently combine. Set aside.

Combine the flour, spices and salt in a bowl. Place the egg and breadcrumbs in separate bowls.

Dip a fish strip in the flour mixture, dusting off any excess, then dip into the egg, letting the excess drip off and finally coat in the breadcrumbs. Place on a tray and repeat with the remaining fish strips. Loosely cover and chill the crumbed fish for 10–15 minutes (this helps keep the fish moist and stops it from over-cooking).

Half-fill a saucepan with oil and place over medium–high heat to bring it to 190°C or until a cube of bread dropped in the oil browns in 10–15 seconds. Fry the fish for 45–75 seconds until golden. Remove and place on paper towel to drain.

Divide the tortillas among serving plates, add a little cabbage and lettuce, then top with the fish. Finish with some salsa and a drizzle of smoked mayo.

THE MOST SIMPLE AND DELICIOUS THINGS IN LIFE?

- A snag from Bunnings
- 3 am water next to the bed
- Someone else's hot chips
- The slivers of cake you keep sneaking
- The first piece of anything your mum gives you while she's cooking
- The first thing a date cooks for you
- The rolls/sandwiches you get at school camp
- Getting a text back straight away
- The first drink you get with a new love interest
- Anything involving a group of friends.

5 BASIC AF VIETNAMESE VERMICELLI SALADS

VERMICELLI SALAD

This simple vermicelli salad is your starting point to make my 5 basic AF salads. It's also a delicious salad on its own, with fragrant herbs, crunchy nuts and veg, and tangy nuoc mam.

SERVES 2

150 g cooked vermicelli noodles
½ carrot, finely sliced into batons
½ Lebanese cucumber, finely sliced into batons
4 cos lettuce leaves, roughly chopped
½ cup bean sprouts
½ cup shredded red cabbage
1 bunch of mint, leaves picked
1 bunch of coriander, leaves picked
1 bunch of Vietnamese mint, leaves picked

TO SERVE
Nuoc Mam Dipping Sauce (page 34)
Salted Peanuts (page 26)
lime cheeks

Combine the noodles, carrot, cucumber, lettuce, bean sprouts and cabbage in a mixing bowl.

In another bowl, mix the mint, coriander and Vietnamese mint.

All you have to do now is divide each mixture into two bowls (herbs on top) and dress with the nuoc mam and some salted peanuts. Serve with lime wedges and whichever protein choice from the five options to follow that take your fancy.

1. GRILLED PORK MEATBALLS

BUN CHA

I'd say bun cha is maybe the third most well-known Vietnamese dish and it's like our answer to a burger … well, kinda. I had a love–hate relationship with bun cha for years because, like, I didn't grow up eating it and, being a Scorpio I *hate* being wrong … So, when friends who came back from the north of Vietnam were all like, 'Bun cha is lit.' I would be like, 'Nah, but have you had bun thit nuong?'

Anyway, after a few tries of bun cha, I finally understood and learned to see the beauty in the dish. While it would make the recipe a lot less basic, cooking the patties on a charcoal barbecue (see page 12) will take this dish to a whole other level: think fat dripping on the coals, sizzling and causing small fires and puffs of sexy smoke infusing the meat. STOP! EVERYTHING! MAKE THESE NOW! KTHXBYE!

P.S. Bun thit nuong is still the bomb – see page 218 for my recipe.

SERVES 2

300 g fatty pork mince
1 tablespoon fish sauce
2 teaspoons finely chopped
   lemongrass
3 tablespoons finely chopped spring
   onion (white part only)
1 garlic clove, crushed
1 tablespoon finely chopped
   coriander stems
1 egg, lightly beaten
2 teaspoons caster sugar
½ teaspoon ground white pepper
pinch of sea salt
2 tablespoons vegetable oil
Vermicelli Salad (page 213)

Combine the pork, fish sauce, lemongrass, spring onion, garlic, coriander stem, egg, sugar, pepper and salt in a large bowl and mix well.

Shape the mixture into ten equal-sized meatballs, then squish them a little into patties. Place on a plate lined with baking paper, cover and refrigerate for 10 minutes.

Heat a large frying pan over medium heat and add 1 tablespoon of the vegetable oil. Cook five of the patties for 2–3 minutes until golden. Flip and cook for a further 2 minutes, then remove. Repeat with the remaining oil and patties.

Serve with the vermicelli salad.

PICTURED ON PAGE 217

2. SPRING ROLLS

BUN CHA GIO

This salad is the most basic of all five as it actually uses the spring rolls from page 33. All you have to do is chop them up with scissors and chuck them on top of your vermicelli salad. It's a great way to use up leftover springs rolls for lunch the next day (usually I don't have leftover spring rolls, though). Of course, if you don't feel like making the vermicelli salad, you can just wrap them up with a truckload of herbs in a lettuce leaf like in the sexy picture below.

PICTURED WITH VERMICELLI SALAD ON PAGE 216

GRILLED PORK MEATBALLS

SPRING ROLLS (PAGE 215)

AKA BUN CHA (PAGE 214)

3. CHARRED MARINATED PORK

BUN THIT NUONG

Bun thit nuong is the bee's knees. Flavourful, aromatic and absolutely appropriate for all occasions. Big call, I know, but THIS IS THE BOMBBBBB! The first time I had this in Vietnam, I was throwing a hissy fit on the side of the road because we couldn't find a certain banh mi ... I was 11 years old and hangry (not much has changed). My mum got a skewer of pork for me from a bun thit nuong vendor and I ended up asking for five more skewers. For this recipe I use a chargrill pan but if you want to thread the pork onto skewers and cook them over coals, you'll really understand the full deliciousness that is bun thit nuong.

SERVES 2

500 g boneless pork shoulder, cut into 1 cm thick slices, then into 3 cm pieces (boneless pork belly will work, too, just remove the skin)
2 tablespoons vegetable oil
Vermicelli Salad (page 213)

MARINADE
2 tablespoons caster sugar
1 lemongrass stalk, very finely chopped
2 garlic cloves, crushed
5 spring onions, white parts only, pounded into a paste with a mortar and pestle
2 teaspoons honey
2 teaspoons kecap manis
2 teaspoons dark soy sauce
1 red shallot, very finely chopped
1 teaspoon sesame oil
1 teaspoon freshly ground black pepper
pinch of sea salt

Combine all the marinade ingredients in a mixing bowl. Add the pork and mix well to coat. Cover and leave to marinate in the fridge for 1 hour.

Heat 2 teaspoons of the vegetable oil in a chargrill pan over high heat. Once the pan is hot, add a quarter of the marinated pork and cook for 2 minutes. Flip and cook for a further 90 seconds. You want the pork to be beautifully caramelised and charred. If you have a charcoal barbecue, you can use it to cook the pork (see page 12). If you don't have one, you can hit the pork with a blowtorch just to get it nice and smoky.

Repeat with the remaining oil and pork, set aside to cool a little, then serve on top of your vermicelli salad.

PICTURED ON PAGE 221

4. LEMONGRASS CHICKEN

BUN GA XAO SA OT

Lemongrass chicken is wonderful with vermicelli salad. The hum of heat from the chilli and the perfect balance of salty, sweet and sour will keep you coming back for more. The marinade is versatile, so you can swap out the chicken for beef, pork, tofu or even tempeh. I usually make this in bulk and freeze it in single-serve portions ready to be defrosted and cooked, perfect for any salad or even in sandwiches.

SERVES 2

200 g skin-on chicken thigh fillets
Vermicelli Salad (page 213)

MARINADE

1 garlic clove, crushed
1 red shallot, very finely chopped
1 tablespoon lime juice
1 tablespoon fish sauce
2 teaspoons light soy sauce
1 tablespoon brown sugar
1 tablespoon peanut oil
1 lemongrass stalk, finely chopped
1 long red chilli, chopped
pinch of sea salt

Combine all the marinade ingredients in a zip-lock bag. Add the chicken, seal and shake it around to mix well. Leave to marinate in the fridge for 30 minutes, or overnight if you want to really let it do its job.

Heat a large chargrill pan over medium heat. Give the chicken thigh fillets a bit of a shake to remove excess marinade before placing them in the pan. Cook for 4–6 minutes on each side until charred (the brown sugar will really help the chicken caramelise), then rest for 5 minutes before slicing.

Serve on top of the vermicelli salad.

PICTURED ON PAGE 221

5. MARINATED MUSHROOMS

BUN NAM

I came up with this recipe when I tried to go vegan in 2015. I was missing my vermicelli salads and needed my fix. It's sweet and salty and the caramelised mushrooms give the dish a smoky flavour that reminds me of bun thit nuong. Great to make on food prep days, you can even have the mushrooms as part of a breakfast fry-up – just drop the vermicelli salad.

SERVES 2

2–3 large portobello mushrooms, halved
2 tablespoons sesame oil
3 tablespoons soy sauce
1 tablespoon kecap manis
2 teaspoons brown sugar
2 garlic cloves, crushed
2 cm piece of ginger, grated
2 red shallots, finely sliced
juice of ½ lime
pinch of sea salt
Vermicelli Salad (page 213)

Place all the ingredients except the salad in a zip-lock bag and combine well, massaging the mushroom with your fingers through the bag (weird, but it helps). Leave for at least 30 minutes for the mushroom to soak up the marinade.

Heat a large chargrill pan over high heat and sear the mushroom for 3 minutes on each side so you get nice char lines on the mushies.

Remove and slice the mushroom into 1 cm thick pieces and serve on top of your vermicelli salad.

MARINATED MUSHROOMS

LEMONGRASS
CHICKEN

CHARRED MARINATED PORK

3PM PROTEIN BALLS

I used to be so confused about protein balls and how they worked. If they are raw, how do they stay together? Makes no sense. That seems hard. It's witchcraft. It's not for me. Well, I was wrong. It is not hard, they set and stay together due to the natural fats and sugars, and they are definitely for me. Most days I have a random moment when I'm starving but it's not dinner time and I just need something to tide me over. For me a protein ball has it all – texture, sweetness, saltiness and enough yum to keep me going. Give these a go, as they are nutritious, perfect to pack into lunch boxes and don't die while you're trying to transport them.

MAKES 16

- 60 g (1 cup) shredded coconut, plus extra for rolling
- 125 g (½ cup) crunchy peanut butter
- 110 g (⅔ cup) roasted peanuts
- 60 g (⅓ cup) medjool dates, pitted
- 3 tablespoons chocolate-flavoured protein powder
- 3 tablespoons chia seeds (whatever colour you want)
- ½ teaspoon sea salt
- 2 tablespoons melted coconut oil

How easy is this? Pop everything except the coconut oil in a food processor and pulse until the peanuts are still just visible (about the texture of very coarse sand). Add the coconut oil and pulse until just combined.

Shape the mixture into 16 balls, then roll in the extra coconut. Place in an airtight container and refrigerate until firm.

These protein balls will keep in the fridge in their airtight container for up to 1 week. Take them to work with you but maybe only take two or three at a time – for some reason they like to go missing.

THE EASIEST CAKE EVER

I used to be shit-scared of baking – like, it has to be so precise, everything needs to be weighed, the methods always confused me – but now I get it. The ratio here always works and it's all about the balance between fat, sugar and starch. Once you get that, you can use this recipe as a base, just like my ice cream recipe on page 180. This cake is foolproof and versatile, perfect for making with kids.

SERVES 8–10

120 g unsalted butter, plus extra
    for greasing
120 g caster sugar
120 g egg (aka 2 eggs)
120 g plain flour, plus extra
    for dusting
1 teaspoon baking powder
pinch of sea salt

Preheat the oven to 180°C. Grease a 20 cm round cake tin with butter and dust the inside with flour.

Place the butter, sugar and eggs in the bowl of a stand mixer fitted with the paddle attachment and beat on high for 3–5 minutes until thick and glossy.

Meanwhile, in a large bowl, sift the flour, baking powder and salt together. Gradually fold the dry ingredients into the wet ingredients, then pour the batter into the prepared tin, shaking gently to make sure everything settles. Bake for 30–40 minutes until a skewer inserted into the centre comes out clean.

Cool the cake in the tin for 10 minutes, then turn out onto a wire rack to cool completely.

CHOOSE YOUR FLAVOUR!

VANILLA

Add 2 teaspoons of vanilla bean paste to the mixer with the butter, sugar and eggs.

CHOCOLATE

When sifting the dry ingredients, subtract 10 g of flour and add 20 g of cocoa powder.

HAZELNUT

Before pouring the batter into the cake tin, fold through 80 g of hazelnuts that have been lightly bashed with the side of a knife.

APPLE AND CINNAMON

Peel and chop 2 granny smith apples into wedges and arrange on the bottom of the greased and floured cake tin. When sifting the dry ingredients, add 1 teaspoon of ground cinnamon.

BEING BASIC: SIMPLE AND HEALTHY EATS FOR EVERY DAY

MATCHA and RASPBERRY RAW SLICE

This slice happened when friends of mine who own @matcha_maiden sent me a pack of their wonderful matcha green tea powder. I knew I was going to be on the podcast @seize_the_yay with one of the owners, and decided to bring some treats along. Knowing she was gluten free and owned a vegan cafe, I challenged myself to make a gluten-free, vegan, raw dessert (I know you're thinking eeew, but this is really good). The tang of the freeze-dried raspberries perfectly balances the creamy nuts and herbaceous green tea flavour, and it's sweetened with dates and rice malt syrup. This treat is absolutely a hipster's dream.

MAKES 16

310 g (2 cups) raw cashews, soaked in water overnight and drained
125 ml (½ cup) canned coconut milk
80 ml (⅓ cup) melted coconut oil
125 ml (½ cup) rice malt syrup
2 tablespoons lemon juice
2 teaspoons vanilla bean paste
pinch of sea salt
1 tablespoon matcha powder, plus extra to serve
10 g (⅓ cup) freeze-dried raspberries, plus extra to serve

CRUST
90 g walnuts
100 g (1 cup) almond meal
5 medjool dates, pitted
3 tablespoons coconut oil
½ teaspoon sea salt

Grease a 20 cm square cake tin and line with baking paper.

First, we'll make the crust. Place all the ingredients in a food processor and blitz until it comes together into a sticky dough that still has visible pieces of walnut (if it looks like nut butter, you've gone too far). Press the dough evenly into the base of the tin, then set aside.

Clean out the food processor bowl, then add the cashews, coconut milk, coconut oil, rice malt syrup, lemon juice, vanilla and salt. Blitz till smooth and creamy. Remove one-third of the mixture and set aside. Add the matcha powder to the processor, then blitz until combined.

Spread the matcha filling evenly into the tin on top of the crust, cover and place in the freezer.

Clean the food processor bowl again, pop in the reserved filling mixture along with the freeze-dried raspberries, then blitz till combined. Pour the raspberry mixture over the top of the matcha filling, cover again and return to the freezer for about 3 hours or until completely frozen.

When you are ready to serve, remove from the freezer and slice into 16 pieces. Top with a few extra freeze-dried raspberries and some matcha powder.

CONVERSION CHARTS

Measuring cups and spoons may vary slightly from one country to another, but the difference is generally not enough to affect a recipe. All cup and spoon measures are level.

One Australian metric measuring cup holds 250 ml (8 fl oz), one Australian metric tablespoon holds 20 ml (4 teaspoons) and one Australian metric teaspoon holds 5 ml. North America, New Zealand and the UK use a 15 ml (3-teaspoon) tablespoon.

LENGTH

METRIC	IMPERIAL
3 mm	⅛ inch
6 mm	¼ inch
1 cm	½ inch
2.5 cm	1 inch
5 cm	2 inches
18 cm	7 inches
20 cm	8 inches
23 cm	9 inches
25 cm	10 inches
30 cm	12 inches

LIQUID MEASURES

ONE AMERICAN PINT	ONE IMPERIAL PINT
500 ml (16 fl oz)	600 ml (20 fl oz)

CUP	METRIC	IMPERIAL
⅛ cup	30 ml	1 fl oz
¼ cup	60 ml	2 fl oz
⅓ cup	80 ml	2½ fl oz
½ cup	125 ml	4 fl oz
⅔ cup	160 ml	5 fl oz
¾ cup	180 ml	6 fl oz
1 cup	250 ml	8 fl oz
2 cups	500 ml	16 fl oz
2¼ cups	560 ml	20 fl oz
4 cups	1 litre	32 fl oz

DRY MEASURES

The most accurate way to measure dry ingredients is to weigh them. However, if using a cup, add the ingredient loosely to the cup and level with a knife; don't compact the ingredient unless the recipe requests 'firmly packed'.

METRIC	IMPERIAL
15 g	½ oz
30 g	1 oz
60 g	2 oz
125 g	4 oz (¼ lb)
185 g	6 oz
250 g	8 oz (½ lb)
375 g	12 oz (¾ lb)
500 g	16 oz (1 lb)
1 kg	32 oz (2 lb)

OVEN TEMPERATURES

CELSIUS	FAHRENHEIT
100°C	200°F
120°C	250°F
150°C	300°F
160°C	325°F
180°C	350°F
200°C	400°F
220°C	425°F

CELSIUS	GAS MARK
110°C	¼
130°C	½
140°C	1
150°C	2
170°C	3
180°C	4
190°C	5
200°C	6
220°C	7
230°C	8
240°C	9
250°C	10

THANK YOU!

This book would never have been possible without my family and friends who believed in me no matter how weird and big my ideas were. Thank you for taking time out of your lives to provide advice and also for making yourselves available to be unpaid faces/bodies/hands in these pages.

To my mum Dzung and sister Amy. FML, what would I do without you two? I love you both and thank you for loving me back.

To my housemate and bestie, Diana Chan, thanks for the support and the rendang recipe. And to the KIC girls, Laura Henshaw and Steph Claire Miller, for the cookie recipe.

To my friends Luke, Oskar, Kale and Tara, for providing me with stories to pair with my recipes.

To my exes, for breaking my heart. I hope you read this and be like 'Oh shit, he's killing it'.

To my *MasterChef* crew, judges and competitors for giving me my new career, allowing me to grow and teaching me so much. My experience on the program, I can honestly say, has changed my life.

To my kitchen team on shoot, Emma, Meryl and Sarah, for making my dishes and recipes come to life.

To the wonderful Andy Warren for designing my book – you rock!

To Lauren Bamford, thank you for the incredible photography that has lifted my food right off the page.

To Deb Kaloper, you absolute gun. I have never seen a stylist so organised and with such amazing vision – you've made my food so sexy.

To my Plum/Pan Macmillan family, Mary, Jane and Ashley. Working with you incredible women has been an absolute joy. You've let my idea come to life, you've let me do me, you've believed in my book from day one and you've made me an author, which I will forever be thankful for.

Finally, to my readers, this was for you. Thank you for reading, cooking and eating the recipes in this book. Thank you for letting me share *A Gay Guy's Guide* with you. Here is to hopefully many more books to come.

INDEX

2-minute mayo.........................151
3 basic AF rice paper
    rolls........................... 200–1
3 pm protein balls 223
5 basic AF Vietnamese
    vermicelli salads...........213–20

A

After-school prawns and
    pork belly............................48
anchovies: My spag bol...........78
annatto seeds 61
Apple and cinnamon cake...224
avocado
    Crispy fish tacos 208
    Millennial chicken salad ... 198
    salsa.................................... 208
    Smashed avo and
        poachies 191
    Tuna and wasabi ponzu
        rice paper rolls 201
    Vegan rainbow rice paper
        rolls....................................201

B

Baked brie with rosemary
    and figs................................67
Balinese coconut and snake
    bean salad 116
banana blossoms 61
    Hue-style beef noodle
        soup 60
Banana fritters........................90
Bang bang Sichuan
    chicken............................... 118
Banh xeo................................ 37
Bap nuong mo hanh..................22
beans: Balinese coconut
    and snake bean salad........ 116

beef
    Beef noodle soup 46
    Beef wrapped in betel
        leaf.................................... 26
    broth..................................... 61
    Cheeseburger spring rolls..68
    Hue-style beef noodle
        soup 60
    Malaysian beef rendang....88
    My spag bol 78
    Shaking beef 174
    Spaghetti for one 121
    Steak and chimi 126
Beef noodle soup.......................46
Beef wrapped in betel leaf....26
beetroot: End-of-the-week
    roast veg 196
betel leaves 26
    Beef wrapped in betel
        leaf.................................... 26
blackberries: Kladdkaka.........98
blood orange dressing...........155
Bo la lot......................................26
bread, Sweet and tangy
    strawberry 138
brie, Baked, with rosemary
    and figs............................... 67
broccoli
    Healthy fried 'rice' 195
    Millennial chicken salad ... 198
    Thai green curry....................160
broth..61
brussels sprouts: End-of-
    the-week roast veg.............196
buckwheat: Millennial
    chicken salad 198
Bun bo hue..................................60
Bun cha......................................214
Bun cha gio................................215
Bun ga xao sa ot.......................219
Bun nam................................... 220
Bun thit nuong...........................218

C

Ca phe sua da.............................20
cabbage
    Charred marinated pork
        vermicelli salad.................218
    Chicken congee with
        crunchy cabbage
        salad..................................123
    Crispy fish tacos 208
    Grilled pork meatballs
        vermicelli salad.................214
    Lemongrass chicken
        vermicelli salad.................219
    Marinated mushrooms
        vermicelli salad 220
    Spring rolls vermicelli
        salad..................................215
    Vegan rainbow rice
        paper rolls 201
    Vermicelli salad.....................213
    Your new favourite
        charred cabbage 194
Cacio e pepe 105
cakes
    Kladdkaka 98
    The easiest cake ever.........224
capers, crispy 169
capsicum
    (Kinda) greek salad............ 205
    Post-gym eggs 188
    Roasted capsicum dip 147
    Shaking beef 174
    Thai green curry....................160
caramel, whisky 183
caramel, peanut butter..........139
carrots
    Balinese coconut and
        snake bean salad 116
    Charred marinated pork
        vermicelli salad.................218

Chicken congee with crunchy cabbage salad 123
Crispy pork belly and ribbon salad 172
End-of-the-week roast veg 196
Grilled pork meatballs vermicelli salad 214
Lemongrass chicken vermicelli salad 219
Marinated mushrooms vermicelli salad 220
My spag bol 78
Pork and fennel ragu for you 86
Pork, ginger and lime sausage rolls 72
Prawn and pork spring rolls 33
Rice paper rolls with prawn and pork 200
Spring rolls vermicelli salad 215
Vegan rainbow rice paper rolls 201
Vegemite and chicken dumplings 168
Vermicelli salad 213

cauliflower
End-of-the-week roast veg 196
Healthy fried 'rice' 195
Sriracha and coconut cauliflower 157

celery
My spag bol 78
Pork and fennel ragu for you 86
Vegemite and chicken dumplings 168
Cha gio tom thit 33
Chao goi ga 123
Charred marinated pork 218

cheese
Baked brie with rosemary and figs 67
Cacio e pepe 105
Cheeseburger spring rolls 68

Gnocchi for gays 83
(Kinda) greek salad 205
Lovers' salad 155
Millennial chicken salad 198
My spag bol 78
Naughty crispy potatoes 115
Pork and fennel ragu for you 86
Post-gym eggs 188
Smashed avo and poachies 191
Spaghetti for one 121
Walnut and blue cheese salad 152
Cheeseburger spring rolls 68
Cherry and coconut slice 94

chicken
Bang bang Sichuan chicken 118
Chicken congee with crunchy cabbage salad 123
Chicken noodle soup 52
Chinese chicken and corn egg-drop soup 106
Lemongrass chicken vermicelli salad 219
Millennial chicken salad 198
Thai green curry 160
The easiest fried chicken ever 206
Vegemite and chicken dumplings 168
Chicken congee with crunchy cabbage salad 123
Chicken noodle soup 52
chickpeas: Hummus 146
chilli strands, fried 162
chimichurri 126
Chinese celery 57
Chinese chicken and corn egg-drop soup 106

chocolate
Cherry and coconut slice 94
Chocolate cake 224
'Keep it cleaner' choc chip cookies 93
Kladdkaka 98
Sexy chocolate comb 179

Wickedly good 'snickers' tart 139
Chocolate cake 224
Choose-your-own ice cream 180
Chuoi chien 90
Cinnamon ice cream 181
clams: Lemongrass and sake clams 58

coconut
3 pm protein balls 223
Balinese coconut and snake bean salad 116
Cherry and coconut slice 94
Crispy Vietnamese pancakes 37
Dhal pasta for my darls 75
Malaysian beef rendang 88
Matcha and raspberry raw slice 226
Sriracha and coconut cauliflower 157
Thai green curry 160
coffee, Vietnamese iced, aka the best coffee in the world 20
congee, Chicken, with crunchy cabbage salad 123
cook's notes 12
cookies, 'Keep it cleaner' choc chip 93

corn
Chinese chicken and corn egg-drop soup 106
Healthy fried 'rice' 195
Salted caramel popcorn 128
Streetside corn on the cob 22
crab: Tamarind crab 51
crepes, Sunday 130
crispy capers 169
Crispy fish tacos 208
Crispy pork belly and ribbon salad 172
Crispy Vietnamese pancakes 37
Cua rang me 51

cucumber
Bang bang Sichuan chicken 118

Charred marinated pork vermicelli salad.......218

Crispy pork belly and ribbon salad......................172

Grilled pork meatballs vermicelli salad.................214

(Kinda) greek salad............205

Lemongrass chicken vermicelli salad.................219

Marinated mushrooms vermicelli salad...............220

Mum's sweet and sour squid..................................57

Rice paper rolls with prawn and pork..............200

Spring rolls vermicelli salad..........................215

Tuna and wasabi ponzu rice paper rolls.................201

Vegan rainbow rice paper rolls..........................201

Vermicelli salad......................213

curry paste, green...................160

curry powder, Malaysian........89

curry, Thai green.......................160

D

daikon

Chicken congee with crunchy cabbage salad......................................123

Chicken noodle soup...........52

dashi..74

dates

3 pm protein balls.................223

'Keep it cleaner' choc chip cookies.........................93

Matcha and raspberry raw slice...........................226

My drunk and sticky date.................................183

Dhal pasta for my darls............75

Diep nuong mo hanh.................25

dips

Hummus...................................146

Mushroom pate.....................147

Roasted capsicum dip...............................147

dipping sauces...........................174

Nuoc mam dipping sauce..34

peanut dipping sauce........201

secret dipping sauce...........68

wasabi ponzu dipping sauce..201

see also sauces

dressing, blood orange......155

dumplings, Vegemite and chicken...............................168

E

eggs

2-minute mayo.......................151

Chinese chicken and corn egg-drop soup.......106

Choose-your-own ice cream......................................180

Furikake omelette rice.........74

Healthy fried 'rice'...............195

(Kinda) greek salad............205

Post-gym eggs......................188

Smashed avo and poachies.............................191

End-of-the-week roast veg..196

essential ingredients.................13

F

fennel: End-of-the-week roast veg......................196

figs: Baked brie with rosemary and figs.................67

fish

Crispy fish tacos.................208

see also anchovies, tuna

Five-spice school prawns.......30

fried chilli strands......................162

furikake.......................................74

Furikake omelette rice.........74

G

Gnocchi for gays........................83

Goi ngo sen................................45

green curry paste.....................160

Green curry prawn toast with sriracha mayo..............162

Grilled occy and crispy capers.....................................169

Grilled pork meatballs............214

Grilled scallops with spring onion oil.......................................25

Grilled sugarcane prawns....110

H

Hazelnut cake..........................224

Healthy fried 'rice'....................195

Honey ice cream.......................181

Hue-style beef noodle soup...60

Hummus.......................................146

i

ice cream: Choose-your-own ice cream.......................180

iced coffee, Vietnamese, aka the best coffee in the world..20

ingredients, essential................13

K

kale: Dhal pasta for my darls...75

karamel masakan.......................89

'Keep it cleaner' choc chip cookies....................................93

(Kinda) greek salad...............205

Kladdkaka.....................................98

L

Lemongrass and sake clams..58

Lemongrass chicken...............219

lentils: Dhal pasta for my darls...75

lime mayo.......................................30

lotus stems...................................44

Prawn and lotus stem
    salad.................................45
Lovers' salad................................155

M

Malaysian beef rendang........88
mam ruoc hue 61
marinades.......................... 218, 219
Marinated mushrooms.......... 220
Matcha and raspberry
    raw slice.................................226
mayonnaise
    2-minute mayo 151
    lime mayo.................................30
    smoked mayo........................ 208
    sriracha mayo.........................162
Millennial chicken salad........ 198
Muc xao thom............................. 57
Mum's sweet and sour
    squid....................................... 57
mushrooms
    Marinated mushrooms
        vermicelli salad................ 220
    Mushroom pate.....................147
    Prawn and pork spring
        rolls 33
    Spring rolls vermicelli
        salad...................................215
Mushroom pate 147
My drunk and sticky date......183
My spag bol 78

N

Naughty crispy potatoes 115
Ngheu hap sa...............................58
noodles
    Beef noodle soup 46
    Charred marinated pork
        vermicelli salad.................218
    Chicken noodle soup........... 52
    Grilled pork meatballs
        vermicelli salad.................214
    Hue-style beef noodle
        soup 60
    Lemongrass chicken
        vermicelli salad.................219

Marinated mushrooms
    vermicelli salad................ 220
Rice paper rolls with
    prawn and pork 200
Smoky sriracha noods 109
Spring rolls vermicelli
    salad.................................215
Tuna and wasabi ponzu
    rice paper rolls 201
Vegan rainbow rice paper
    rolls 201
Vermicelli salad....................213
Nuoc mam...................................34
Nuoc mam dipping sauce.......34
nuts
    3 pm protein balls.................223
    Chicken congee with
        crunchy cabbage
        salad.................................123
    Grilled scallops with
        spring onion oil................. 25
    Hazelnut cake 224
    'Keep it cleaner' choc
        chip cookies 93
    (Kinda) greek salad............ 205
    Matcha and raspberry
        raw slice...........................226
    Millennial chicken salad ... 198
    Mushroom pate.....................147
    peanut dipping sauce........ 201
    Prawn and lotus stem
        salad................................... 45
    Roasted capsicum dip 147
    salted peanuts........................ 26
    Smoky sriracha noods 109
    Sriracha and coconut
        cauliflower 157
    Thai green curry...................160
    Vegan rainbow rice paper
        rolls 201
    Walnut and blue cheese
        salad.................................152
    Wickedly good 'snickers'
        tart.......................................139
    Your new favourite charred
        cabbage 194

O

octopus: Grilled occy and
    crispy capers.......................... 169
oils
    spiced oil.................................60
    spring onion oil...................... 25
omelette, Furikake, rice 74
onions, vinegar 52
onions, vinegar red...................174
oranges
    blood orange dressing 155
    Lovers' salad..........................155
    Tuna and wasabi ponzu
        rice paper rolls 201
    wasabi ponzu dipping
        sauce 201
oregano 205

P

pancakes
    Crispy Vietnamese
        pancakes 37
    Sunday crepes...................... 130
pasta
    Cacio e pepe.......................... 105
    Dhal pasta for my darls 75
    My spag bol 78
    Pork and fennel ragu for
        you...86
    Spaghetti for one 121
pate, Mushroom 147
peanut butter caramel...........139
Peanut butter ice cream........181
peanut dipping sauce............ 201
peanuts, salted........................ 26
pears: Walnut and blue
    cheese salad.........................152
peas
    Healthy fried 'rice' 195
    Thai green curry....................160
Pho bo..46
Pho ga.. 52
pickled chilli 53
pineapple
    broth.. 61
    Hue-style beef noodle
        soup 60

Mum's sweet and sour squid 57
pomegranate: Lovers' salad 155
popcorn, Salted caramel 128

pork
After-school prawns and pork belly...........................48
Beef wrapped in betel leaf.....................................26
broth..61
Charred marinated pork vermicelli salad.................218
Cheeseburger spring rolls 68
Crispy pork belly and ribbon salad......................172
Crispy Vietnamese pancakes 37
Grilled pork meatballs vermicelli salad.................214
Healthy fried 'rice' 195
Hue-style beef noodle soup 60
My spag bol 78
Naughty crispy potatoes....115
Pork and fennel ragu for you.......................................86
Pork, ginger and lime sausage rolls 72
Prawn and pork spring rolls 33
Rice paper rolls with prawn and pork 200
Smoky sriracha noods 109
Spring rolls vermicelli salad 215
Pork and fennel ragu for you.......................................86
Pork, ginger and lime sausage rolls 72
Post-gym eggs.......................188

potatoes
Gnocchi for gays 83
Naughty crispy potatoes............................115
Prawn and lotus stem salad 45
Prawn and pork spring rolls...33

prawns
After-school prawns and pork belly...........................48
Crispy Vietnamese pancakes 37
Five-spice school prawns...................................30
Green curry prawn toast with sriracha mayo..........162
Grilled sugarcane prawns.................................110
Prawn and lotus stem salad 45
Prawn and pork spring rolls 33
Rice paper rolls with prawn and pork 200
Spring rolls vermicelli salad 215
protein balls, 3 pm 223
pudding: My drunk and sticky date...............................183

R

radishes: Crispy pork belly and ribbon salad.................172
ragu, Pork and fennel, for you 86
raspberries: Matcha and raspberry raw slice 226
Rau muong xao toi 40
rendang, Malaysian beef 88
ribbon salad.................................172

rice paper rolls
Rice paper rolls with prawn and pork 200
Tuna and wasabi ponzu rice paper rolls 201
Vegan rainbow rice paper rolls 201
Rice paper rolls with prawn and pork.................................200

rice
Chicken congee with crunchy cabbage salad...............................123
Furikake omelette rice 74
Thai green curry...................160

Roasted capsicum dip.............147
rock sugar...................................47

S

sake: Lemongrass and sake clams..58

salads
Balinese coconut and snake bean salad 116
Charred marinated pork vermicelli salad.................218
Crispy pork belly and ribbon salad......................172
Grilled pork meatballs vermicelli salad.................214
(Kinda) greek salad...........205
Lemongrass chicken vermicelli salad.................219
Lovers' salad...........................155
Marinated mushrooms vermicelli salad...............220
Millennial chicken salad ... 198
Prawn and lotus stem salad 45
Spring rolls vermicelli salad 215
Vermicelli salad......................213
Walnut and blue cheese salad 152
salsa 208
Salted caramel popcorn 128
salted peanuts.........................26

sauces
chimichurri..............................126
salsa 208
Sichuan sauce 118
see also dipping sauces, mayonnaise
sausage rolls, Pork, ginger and lime 72
scallops: Grilled scallops with spring onion oil..............25
seafood *see* clams, crabs, octopus, prawns, scallops, squid
seasoning, super-simple......206
secret dipping sauce 68
Sexy chocolate comb 179

Shaking beef 174
shrimp paste 61
Sichuan sauce........................... 118
slices
   Cherry and coconut slice ...94
   Matcha and raspberry
     raw slice..............................226
Smashed avo and
   poachies.................................191
smoked mayo 208
Smoky sriracha noods............109
soups
   Beef noodle soup 46
   Chicken noodle soup............ 52
   Chinese chicken and
     corn egg-drop soup 106
   Hue-style beef noodle
     soup..60
Spaghetti for one......................121
spice paste 88
spiced oil......................................60
spinach
   Hue-style beef noodle
     soup 60
   Stir-fried water spinach
     with garlic 40
spring onion oil 25
Spring rolls.................................215
spring rolls
   Cheeseburger spring
     rolls 68
   Prawn and pork spring
     rolls 33
   Spring rolls vermicelli
     salad.....................................215
squid: Mum's sweet and sour
   squid... 57
Sriracha and coconut
   cauliflower 157
sriracha mayo 162
Steak and chimi.......................126
Stir-fried water spinach
   with garlic................................40
stir-fries
   Five-spice school
     prawns....................................30
   Stir-fried water spinach
     with garlic 40
   After-school prawns and
     pork belly...............................48

Mum's sweet and sour
   squid... 57
   Smoky sriracha noods 109
   Shaking beef 174
   Healthy fried 'rice' 195
strawberries
   Lovers' salad...........................155
   Sweet and tangy
     strawberry bread 138
Streetside corn on the
   cob 22
sugarcane....................................111
Sunday crepes 130
super-simple seasoning....... 206
Sweet and tangy
   strawberry bread 138
Sweet potatoes: End-of-
   the-week roast veg.............196

T

tacos, Crispy fish..................... 208
Tamarind crab............................. 51
tart, Wickedly good
   'snickers'................................139
Thai green curry......................160
The easiest cake ever 224
The easiest fried chicken
   ever 206
toast, Green curry prawn,
   with sriracha mayo 162
tofu: Vegan rainbow rice
   paper rolls 201
Tom rang ngu vi huong 30
Tom rang thit ba roi...................48
tomatoes
   Crispy fish tacos 208
   Dhal pasta for my darls 75
   (Kinda) greek salad............ 205
   Mum's sweet and sour
     squid 57
   My spag bol 78
   salsa 208
   Shaking beef 174
   Spaghetti for one 121
tuna
   (Kinda) greek salad............ 205
   Tuna and wasabi ponzu
     rice paper rolls 201

Tuna and wasabi ponzu rice
   paper rolls 201

V

Vanilla cake................................224
Vanilla ice cream 181
Vegan rainbow rice paper
   rolls.. 201
Vegemite and chicken
   dumplings 168
Vermicelli salad 213
Vietnamese iced coffee
   aka the best coffee in the
   world..20
vinegar onions 52
vinegar red onion....................174

W

Walnut and blue cheese
   salad 152
wasabi ponzu dipping sauce ....
   201
water spinach *see* spinach
whisky caramel 183
Wickedly good 'snickers'
   tart 139

Y

Your new favourite charred
   cabbage.................................. 194

Z

zucchini: Thai green curry.....160

A Plum book

First published in 2020 by
Pan Macmillan Australia Pty Limited
Level 25, 1 Market Street,
Sydney, NSW, Australia 2000

Level 3, 112 Wellington Parade,
East Melbourne, Victoria, Australia 3002

Design by Andy Warren
Typesetting by Megan Ellis
Editing by Hannah Koelmeyer
Index by Helena Holmgren
Photography by Lauren Bamford
Prop and food styling by Deb Kaloper
Food preparation by Emma Warren, Sarah Watson and Meryl Batlle
Colour reproduction by Splitting Image Colour Studio
Printed and bound in China by Imago Printing International Limited

A CIP catalogue record for this book is available from the National
Library of Australia.

10 9 8 7 6 5 4 3